D1554740

2174

## ALSO BY GREG GUTFELD

*The Scorecard:*
*The Official Point System for Keeping*
*Score in the Relationship Game*

# The

# Scorecard

# at Work

# THE
# SCORECARD
# AT WORK

## THE OFFICIAL POINT SYSTEM
## FOR KEEPING SCORE ON THE JOB

**Greg Gutfeld**

An Owl Book

Henry Holt and Company
New York

Henry Holt and Company, Inc.
*Publishers since 1866*
115 West 18th Street
New York, New York 10011

Henry Holt® is a trademark of
Henry Holt and Company, Inc.

Library of Congress Cataloging-in-Publication Data
Gutfeld, Greg.
The scorecard at work : the official point system for keeping score
on the job / Greg Gutfeld.—1st Owl book ed.
p.     cm.—(An owl book)
ISBN 0-8050-5865-6 (pbk. : alk. paper)
1. Career development—Humor.   2. Vocational
guidance—Humor.   I. Title.   II. Series.
HF5381.G923   1999                                          98-35012
650.1′02′07—dc21                                              CIP

Henry Holt books are available for special promotions
and premiums. For details contact: Director, Special Markets.

First Edition 1998

DESIGNED BY BETTY LEW

Printed in the United States of America
All first editions are printed on acid-free paper. ∞

1   3   5   7   9   10   8   6   4   2

# CONTENTS

# ACKNOWLEDGMENTS

Thanks to my family, friends, and all those good people at Wal-Mart. Also thanks to the ever patient Shelia, the industrious group at *Men's Health*, Vern Kordahl (if that's your real name), Golin, Bricklin, Lafavore, Boyles, Geraci, McFadden, Hilton, Gietz, any or all Deslers, and CBS for finally canceling *Murphy Brown*. Also: my ever helpful editor, David Sobel (who clearly needs a vacation), my landlord, Bob Smith (for picking up the beer cans and cigarette butts), the city of Allentown (great water theme park!), and the local paramedics (for reviving me last summer). And finally, to all those hardworking folks at bookstores across the nation who surreptitiously obscure books with "chicken soup" in the title with this one. Well done!

# INTRODUCTION

Despite thousands of career and business books at our finger-tips, not one author has gone to the trouble of telling us how to behave properly in the workplace. True, there are some painfully drab books out there that tell us how to hunt for a job (step one: lose the bathrobe), what to wear at an interview (hint: not the side holster), and how to empower our resumes with senseless action verbs that make us sound like we're channeling Roget. That's it. What we really need is something that helps us assess our behavior at work, telling us when we've screwed up and when we've done well. That way, we'll be golden in the eyes of our bosses, and even better, avoid selling Amway products out of our trunk.

Think about it. From your trumped-up resume (those two years in the Peace Corps were a nice touch!) to the dreadful company picnic (you remember: when you mistakenly thought the egg toss was clothing optional), you're either making smart moves or committing humiliating gaffes. Whatever the case, the workplace is a game. And in this game, you either score points or squander them. In many cases, the points you lose aren't tabulated by an omnipotent being (your lurking boss), but by your coworkers, underlings, interns, and of course, the cafeteria lady who refuses to wear a hair net (it clashes with the Oak Ridge Boys T-shirt).

The workplace is no different than high school. It's a popularity contest where it is more important to be well-liked than it is to hand your work in on time. And these days, it never hurts to be handy with a firearm.

That's why you need this book. The scorecard you hold in your hand will help you chronicle your rise (or fall) in the food chain of cubicle life. The points you earn represent how far you've advanced (or declined) in the eyes of everyone around you. Pull off something clever at work (like coming up with a brilliant marketing slogan for those inflatable loafers), you score big and reap the benefits (a sizable raise, your own parking space, a receptionist who thinks she's a Spice Girl). Do something stupid (lifting that brilliant marketing slogan for those inflatable loafers from *Mein Kampf*) and you fold faster than George Michael at a rest stop bathroom. Worse, if whatever horrible act you commit happens to be recorded by the company security camera, you can kiss that career goodbye (until you're cleared of the charges, of course).

Again, that's why you need this book. It gives you precise measurements (points, my friend, points!) that let you know exactly where you stand in this slippery environment called the workplace. By regularly keeping score, you gain valuable career-building insight few of your coworkers have—the kind of insight that will almost guarantee you more than a 2 percent raise come review time. We're talking at least 2.5 percent!

Of course, there are rules.

**The number of points you score depends on where you are on the corporate ladder.** If you happen to be a new employee, for example, the most important scorekeeper would be your direct supervisor. But as the weeks and months wear on, your fellow employees are also analyzing your performance (as well as your annoying go-getter behavior). It doesn't matter whether they like or dislike you, their main concern is that your hard work and dedication—by comparison—might expose their slapdash work ethic. You can help alleviate this fear, however, by showing up on Casual Friday in a hula skirt.

And while the opinions of your underlings may not count as much as your boss's, they can still do great harm. Maybe not to your career, but to your little Honda Accord in the parking lot. First it will be the tires, then the gas tank, then the brake cable. (This is why I walk to work.)

And, as you move up through the company, the scrutiny—as well as the scoring—becomes more intense. Rise to the level of manager and you'll have to contend with a nervous boss and coworkers who are now resentful, underpaid underlings. They are praying you slip up. And chances are, in time, you will. Especially if you continue to use office mail to deliver crystal meth.

**The points you score have a short shelf life, but the points you lose will make the company newsletter.** Do something great (land that important account), and it's important to cash in fast. Meaning, of course, ask for that raise, a company car, more vacation, or a secretary who cannot bear to see you without a full mug of fresh, hot coffee. Do something profoundly stupid, and, well, no matter what you try to do to earn back respect, you're dog food. You can work nights, work weekends, turn in stellar reports—and you'll always be the person known for counterfeiting twenties on the color copier.

**It is better not to score any points at all than to lose them in one ugly attempt at heroism.** Many business books will tell you that taking risks is the trademark of a truly successful employee. Most of those business books, however, are written by abysmal freaks whose only risk-taking is reflected in their selection of ghoulish hairpieces. Sure, you want to shine. But if shining means going out on a limb, don't bother. Stay in the background and let the other guy make the dumb mistakes. You'll be there to step in and clean up the mess (which, we might add, may require a cursory knowledge in the art of tai kwon do).

**Don't drink decaffeinated coffee.** No one trusts a colleague who doesn't drink the real thing. It's almost as bad as:

- wearing a bow tie to work
- talking about your pets
- showing pictures of your pets
- showing pictures of the Pet of the Year
- borrowing lunch money from coworkers who make less than you
- loudly singing Celine Dion songs while you collate

**Seek every opportunity to upgrade your image, as long as it doesn't appear at the expense of other coworkers.** Let's be clear: we wholeheartedly encourage you to find sneaky, lazy ways to earn points. After all, if you actually try to work hard at your job, you'll have absolutely no time for more interesting endeavors—like playing trash-can basketball or fashioning paper clips into surgical implements. But if your endeavors to elevate yourself are not subtle—say, openly stealing ideas, or worse, spouses—then soon everyone including the cleaning lady will know you're a snake in a sportcoat, and your career will sink faster than a Kevin Costner epic. So be careful out there. Oh, and keep your receipts.

Now, get those pencils ready . . .

# The

# Scorecard

# at Work

# 1 | YOUR RESUME

Resumes are nothing more than the opposite of a rap sheet: a good one chronicles your achievements in a clear, concise (and entirely deceitful) manner. And as long as no one actually checks to see if you really were a rear admiral in the Gulf War, you should do fine. But screw up—by exaggerating, lying, or being just plain sloppy—and you still might find work. The question is, can you support a family making balloon animals at the pier?

- Before you compose your resume, you decide to do some research. **+2**
- You buy resume books to get some helpful tips. **+1**
- Like *Resumes For Dummies.* **-3**
- You follow the examples in the book. **+4**
- You *use* an example. **-23**
- You white-out the page number first. **-55**
- You figure it's easier to change your name than your college transcript. **-76**
- It's the sex change that will be the real challenge. **-211**

- You pay careful attention to spelling errors in your resume. **+3**
- You proofread the resume before sending it out. **+3**

- You retype it several times until it's perfect. **+10**
- You cross out the misspelled words. **-4**
- and write them in correctly above **-17**
- You pencil in the "g" in "manslaughter." **-34**
- with a crayon. **-45**

- You find that there are no misspellings. **+5**
- You can't decide whether "Wal-Mart" is one word or two **-11**
- but you're sure about "San Quentin." **-78**

- Rather than rely on your skills as a proofreader, you also use the computer spellchecker. **+3**
- You rely solely on the computer spellchecker **-5**
- which lets "senile vice president" go through **-34**
- as well as "national seals manager." **-45**
- You're still granted an interview **+4**
- just so the human resources manager can say, "What's up, Flipper?" **-65**
- and toss you a sardine **-80**

- You state your familiarity with all the major software programs **+3**
- like Word, Excel, and WordPerfect **+4**
- not to mention mainframes, minicomputers, and networking hardware. **+6**
- Funny thing is, you only know how much they weigh. **-3**
- It's those fond memories of the shipping department. **-30**

- You use clear, simple sentences to describe your work experience. **+4**
- You overdose on action verbs **-3**
- which you lifted from the resume books. **-5**
- You use words like "empower" and "facilitate" and "systematize" **-8**
- as well as "conceptualize," "expedite," and "formulate." **-13**

- They really raise some eyebrows. **+2**
- You explain that a lot goes into making a Happy Meal. **-34**

- You include a hobbies and special interests section. **-9**
- This is because you have some very intriguing hobbies and special interests. **+2**
- This is because you have no job experience. **-13**
- You collect stamps. **-13**
- You collect baseball cards. **-18**
- You collect baseball players. **-143**
- You recreate Civil War battles on the weekends **-23**
- which will soon become obvious on Casual Friday **-33**
- when you delight us all with your recreation of a bayonet wound **-48**
- as well as the gangrene. **-98**

- You brew your own beer. **+3**
- You have your own still. **-43**
- You make your own explosives. **-333**
- You're wearing them during the interview **-1253**

- You list meaningful accomplishments above and beyond your work experience. **+4**
- You can drive a stick shift. **-32**
- You have a Class 2 license. **-34**
- You can parallel park like a demon. **-44**
- You can hit the porch on a fly from your bicycle. **-87**

- You describe your love for animals. **-3**
- You fail to mention how this got you banned from the zoo. **+2**

- You list a number of achievements bound to impress human resources. **+4**
- You made them all up. **-34**
- But you know they won't check up on it anyway. **+5**
- They're too busy checking your references. **0**

- It will take months for the Pope to get back to them **-23**
- and your mother already used up her one phone call anyway. **-32**

You're a proud graduate of:
- Harvard **+12**
- Yale **+11**
- Sarah Lawrence **+3**
- Sarasota Community College **-5**
- Betty Ford **-32**
- You keep coming back as a "visiting alumnus" **-76**
- in an ambulance. **-250**

- You mention that you once owned your own business. **+6**
- It was a mail-order business. **-9**
- A highly successful mail-order business **+4**
- featuring brides **-34**
- from the Philippines. **-33**
- You're no longer in business, however. **+2**
- You found it demeaning **+3**
- and your inventory got fat. **-99**

- Your resume shows continuous employment since you graduated from college. **+5**
- Well, there are some minor gaps. **-3**
- Actually, there's a three-year gap. **-10**
- You can explain this. **+10**
- You were creating irrigation systems in Angola with the Peace Corps. **+12**
- You were earning your MBA at Harvard. **+15**
- You were watching the NBA at Hooters. **-44**
- You were finding yourself while backpacking through Europe. **-12**
- You returned when the statute of limitations expired **-65**
- or when you ran out of pot. **-100**

- You take extra care in the design of your resume. **+3**
- You use attractive but readable fonts **+2**
- a second color, for emphasis **+2**
- a high-quality stock of paper. **+2**
- After you send it, you quickly get a call from the company's personnel department. **+9**
- They want to know if you do party invitations. **-34**

- You try not to over-sell yourself when describing your qualifications. **+5**
- You exaggerate a bit here and there. **-4**
- You take credit for a number of achievements you had no part in. **-20**
- "I'm sure you've heard of Operation Desert Storm." **-40**
- You take credit for a number of achievements that aren't nearly as notable **-33**
- the metric system **-98**
- the WB network line-up **-112**
- the electric car. **-132**
- You came up with the McDLT. **-123**
- You kept the cold part cold, and the hot part hot. **-143**

- You include a career objective at the beginning of your resume. **+3**
- "Obtaining a senior marketing position for a large publishing company." **+3**
- "Obtaining a job where I am largely unsupervised" **-45**
- "and can expect wonderful gifts from suppliers." **-65**
- "Obtaining a job in pharmaceutical sales" **+2**
- "where I can help better the lives of the sick" **+8**
- "and have easy access to samples" **-32**
- "which will finally get rid of this twitch." **-400**

- You are careful to avoid the typical cliches found in most resumes. **+4**

- You pepper your resume with phrases like "a real team player" **-9**
- as well as "works well with others." **-8**
- Although you've been working out of your home for the last ten years. **-33**
- It's a cabin in the woods. **-40**
- You're still pissed your brother turned you in. **-100**

- You like to call yourself "a people person" **-46**
- because you love being around people **-4**
- and exposing yourself to them **-14**
- on the subway. **-87**
- You call this performance art **-89**
- which could explain the NEA grant. **+23**

- You send your resume by registered mail. **+1**
- You send it by Federal Express. **+3**
- You hand-deliver it to the office. **+4**
- You hand-deliver it to the CEO's house **-13**
- in your underwear **-45**
- at midnight. **-64**
- You apologize for scaring the children. **-75**
- You explain their window was the only one that wasn't locked. **-123**

- For references, you select former supervisors and employees who can honestly attest to your performance on the job. **+3**
- You've worked closely with them on a number of important projects. **+4**
- Who, when called, can't remember you. **-9**
- Who, when called, can't come to the phone **-12**
- because they're "pumping iron in the yard." **-56**

- When your references are contacted, they speak glowingly of you. **+9**

- They begin to mumble nervously. **-34**
- They ask, "When did he get out?" **-75**

- You send out resumes to businesses where your expertise will be appreciated. **+6**
- You send out resumes to anyone with an address. **-23**
- You convince yourself Microsoft could really use someone like you **-33**
- because you used to be an expert at Windows **+2**
- until you lost your squeegie. **-64**

- Under summary of qualifications you list your ten years in corporate sales. **+5**
- You also include your strong presentation and public-speaking skills **+4**
- which you exercised just recently **+5**
- on *Jerry Springer* **-15**
- "Hi, my name is Dave, and it's been six weeks since my last crack binge." **-34**

- Under professional experience, you include technical sales support on innovative new software products. **+4**
- You mention that sales of these products exceeded all company goals. **+7**
- You attribute your success to your special "closer" technique. **+6**
- Some call it extortion. **-34**
- You prefer to call it batting practice **-34**
- since it involves a Louisville Slugger. **-54**

- You orchestrated impressive demonstrations as part of an extensive sales campaign. **+4**
- You created innovative parties to drum up enthusiasm for your products **+3**
- which got a lot of press. **+5**

- The party you threw for your clients made all the papers. **+23**
- That's the last time you hire Heidi Fleiss. **-400**

- You list your long-standing membership in the Audubon Society **+4**
- the United Way **+4**
- The World Wildlife Fund **+8**
- The World Wrestling Federation **-12**
- The Big Brothers of America **+6**
- as well as the National Man-Boy Love Association. **-432**
- You've got show off your date somewhere! **-1000**
- The Hair Club For Men **-24**
- you're not the president **-30**
- just a member **-33**
- which is obvious. **-40**

- Under special talents you write that you are fully experienced in all major software programs. **+4**
- You add that you can choose a fine wine **-5**
- and pry off a non-twist beer bottle cap with your teeth **-12**
- actually, your eye socket. **-43**
- You're great with cars **-5**
- stealing them, actually. **-76**
- You did your own tattoo. **-12**
- You were the best skin artist in prison. **-43**
- Just ask Manson. **-121**
- They will, since he's a reference. **-321**

## SIGNS OF A SCARY RESUME

- any occupation that required showing up at a children's birthday party **-34**
- or a bachelorette party **-15**
- dressed as a cop **-42**
- any occupation that required traveling from small town to small town **-3**
- sharing a trailer with the "Snake Lady" **-45**
- any list of favorite bands **-30**
- or favorite serial killers **-54**
- or favorite Air Supply record **-403**
- hobbies that require knowing where to buy large amounts of fertilizer **-10**
- but have nothing to do with gardening **-1,444**
- "medical schools" from US territories **-34**
- job addresses that are P.O. boxes **-44**
- home addresses that include a cell number **-432**
- "Watching *E.R.*" as post-graduate medical work **-321**
- references from pals **-12**
- references from relatives or next-door neighbors **-30**
- references from pets **-90**
- references from the dead **-140**
- or somebody who goes by the name "Fingers" **-45**
- listing that you played Eddie in *The Munsters* **-40**
- the stage version **-45**
- you were the understudy **-65**
- listing "amateur psychic" under "special talents" **-98**
- taking credit for predicting the break-up of Burt and Loni **-123**
- listing "Commander, Special Forces," under job experience **+3**

- and that you'd be happy to show off the "ten-second chokehold." **-35**
- explaining how you can kill another human being with your little toe **-203**
- mentioning that you're a collector **0**
- and whatever you collect needs to be refrigerated **-303**
- mentioning crime fighting under volunteer work **-245**
- and a willingness to work without a cape **-304**

## THE COVER LETTER

- Your letter specifically targets the prospective employer. **+4**
- Your letter details how your talents are ideally suited to the job. **+5**
- You mention why you wish to leave your present job. **0**
- "No wet bar." **-30**
- You feel the opportunities there are limited. **+3**
- There was just no room for someone like you to grow **+9**
- marijuana on the roof. **-45**

- You spend a paragraph telling the company how much you admire their work. **+2**
- You then tell them how much you can add to their team **+4**
- their marketing team **+5**
- their softball team. **-25**
- You can make it from center field to home on a fly. **-45**
- And you can get 10 percent off on Coors Party Balls. **-48**

- You offer a breezy summary of your career highlights. **+3**
- You mention you helped increased sales profits by 20 percent in two years **+5**
- by taking a sabbatical. **-40**
- You've received numerous awards **+21**
- and citations **+24**

- and a handful of subpoenas. **-45**
- You claim the "real killers" are still out there. **-90**

 # THE INTERVIEW

You've already cleared a major hurdle: fooling that strange character known as the personnel director into thinking you're a viable job candidate (perhaps it was the Garfield sticker on the envelope). Score major points here, and you'll not only win yourself a cubicle but also some really neat office supplies. Don't start stealing those until you know you've got the job (check for security cameras).

## WHAT TO WEAR

- You arrive in your best suit **+5**
- with an impeccable tie and a crisp, white shirt. **+6**
- Actually, it's a novelty tie **-5**
- with neon dancing martini glasses. **-10**
- You believe this will make you stand out from the crowd. **+2**
- It does. **+4**
- The receptionist presses the silent alarm. **-23**

- You wear clothes that best express your personality. **-3**
- You wear a bolo tie because at heart you're just a country boy. **-4**
- You wear a leather coat because you grew up in the mean streets of Brooklyn. **-4**
- You wear a bright orange jumpsuit. **-34**
- It's what you had on when you busted out. **-40**

- You dress conservatively, even though at heart you're not conservative **+3**

- which is why you wore the most discreet nose ring **-19**
- and removed the tongue stud. **+3**
- Now, if you could only cover up that tattoo of Marilyn Manson. **-156**

- You arrive at the interview in a sharp blazer, conservative tie, and a clean, pressed shirt. **+5**
- The interviewer is wearing a polo shirt and jeans. **0**
- So you decide to loosen your tie. **-4**
- The clip-on comes off in your hand. **-12**
- You turn up your collar **-8**
- and roll up your sleeves **-14**
- and roll up a joint **-235**
- and roll up into a ball and fall asleep. **-285**

- You arrive wearing a tasteful, dark pantsuit with an expensive scarf. **+5**
- Actually, you thought you'd arrive wearing something more eye-catching. **-14**
- You wear a sleek white dress **-5**
- which shows off your figure **-6**
- a little too much. **-10**
- You decide to lose the panties and flash him like Sharon Stone in *Basic Instinct*. **-32**
- You realize this would be more effective if you were a woman **-105**
- after about ten minutes. **-226**

## YOUR COMPOSURE

- During the interview, you appear calm and relaxed. **+4**
- You're pleased the Darvon is kicking in. **-44**
- You engage in pleasant small talk with the interviewer. **+3**
- In time you feel relaxed **+5**
- and come in from the ledge. **-64**

- You answer her questions confidently. **+8**
- You begin to feel more assured. **+3**
- You lean back in the chair **-4**
- and put your feet up on the desk. **-20**
- You use her Zen garden for an ashtray. **-34**
- And her aquarium for a snack break. **-74**

<br>

- You pick up a framed picture of her family off the desk **-40**
- and mention how adorable her children are **+3**
- and how it would be shame if anything were to happen to them. **-112**

<br>

- During the interview, you bring up some interesting points about the company. **+3**
- You've clearly done your homework. **+4**
- You comment on how amazing the growth in the overseas market has been **+9**
- and mention your numerous contacts in international markets. **+11**
- Well, cartels, actually. **-23**
- You demonstrate how to conceal contraband in the human body. **-323**

<br>

- You make sure not to mention anything radical or extreme about yourself. **+3**
- You say, "I don't think personal politics have any place in the office." **+4**
- "That's what my fortified cabin in the woods is for." **-40**

<br>

- You refrain from revealing personal information about yourself. **+4**
- You prefer to say, "That's classified." **-44**
- You focus on your relevant skills and experience. **+4**
- You emphasize your unending commitment to working hard. **+4**

- And if he or she is interested, they can call you at their convenience **0**
- but not before noon. **-13**
- "My therapy doesn't end until eleven" **-45**
- "and I need an hour before the drugs kick in." **-65**

- You are currently unemployed, but avoid dwelling on why you aren't working **0**
- or why you got fired. **0**
- "We really don't have to rehash all that ugly business." **-24**
- "Anyone could have made that mistake." **-21**
- "So I mislabeled a few bottles." **-54**
- "It wasn't intentional." **-32**
- "And you might say the Children's Hospital was overcrowded anyway." **-432**

- When the interviewer asks you a difficult question, you pause and think about your response quietly **+1**
- then answer the question articulately. **+4**
- "That's a tough question and I honestly don't know the answer." **0**
- "That's a trick question, right?" **-4**
- "Oh yeah? Well let me ask *you* something!" **-45**

## THE JOB APPLICATION

- On your job application, you leave certain questions blank **-7**
- because you simply can't or don't want to answer them. **-8**
- You fill them in with total fabrications. **-33**
- You figure they really won't check up on your grades in school **-9**

- and whether or not you really did work for the Secret Service. **-33**
- But you are having second thoughts about the Pulitzer **-98**
- and the moon landing. **-132**
- In the box for salary requirements, you simply write, "Open." **+1**
- you write, "Strictly small bills." **-45**

- In the sections asking why you left your previous job, you write, "Looking for more responsibility." **+3**
- You write, "Handwashing policies too strict." **-10**
- You write, "Sheriff closed us down." **-45**
- You write, "Wife found out about Darlene." **-54**

## THE INTERVIEW SIMULATOR

Before you actually attend a real interview, it might help to take a little practice run. This is the same principle medical students use when operating on cadavers, which tend to be only slightly livelier than corporate human resources directors.

1. So, Jerry, tell me about yourself.
- Don't call me Jerry, it's Gerald. **-45**
- It used to be Geraldine. **-150**

2. Okay, Gerald, tell me about yourself.
- I have extensive experience developing and researching marketing strategies, as well as traveling across the country testing new product designs. **+4**
- I'm a real people person! **-6**
- I can play Beethoven's Fifth with my armpit. **-65**
- I'm Batman! **-211**

3· Why weren't your grades better in school?

- I found that "going for grades"—like other students—was not as important as caring for burn victims. **+8**
- My grades weren't that bad, considering how much of the time I was stoned. **-50**
- You got anything to eat? **-84**

4· Why did you major in botany?

- I believe as a people we've neglected the earth, and once the earth declines, so do we. **+6**
- I did what? **-56**
- Let's just say I was kind of an agribusiness entrepreneur **-58**
- especially when the Dead were on tour. **-123**

5· What is your biggest weakness?

- I'm a bit of a perfectionist. And so perhaps I take too much pride in my work. **+3**
- The ponies, man, definitely the ponies. **-45**

6· Why did you stay at your last job so long?

- I was completing advanced degrees at an evening university, and being promoted to more challenging assignments along the way. **+4**
- They kind of forgot about me. **-24**
- I wanted to get vested in my savings plan. **-4**
- They let me sleep there. **-156**

7· Give me an example of a work project that didn't succeed.

- Well, there was one time I was particularly gung ho about a project. I ended up working eighteen-hour days, when I really should have delegated the responsibility. **+6**
- I was Roseanne's personal trainer. **-123**
- I produced *The Hitler Diaries: The Musical.* **-211**
- I once tried to pitch Ellen DeGeneres as a romantic movie lead. **-321**
- Remember the "Lawn Darts for Toddlers" campaign? **-350**

8. So, why advertising?
- It's always been a love of mine, and I enjoy the raw creativity involved in bringing a product to life. **+4**
- You ever watch *Melrose Place*? **-56**

9. Why this company?
- You're at the top of the field, and I only want to work for the best. **+3**
- I heard anything goes at the Christmas party. **-45**
- You're close to the track. **-55**

10. Give me an example of a situation at work that frustrated you.
- When the snowstorm had delayed our shipping, I found alternative ways to get the product out. In the end we met our deadlines. **+9**
- Do you ever get Post-it notes stuck to the bottom of your shoe? **-45**
- The vending machine was out of Ring Dings. **-169**
- It's really frustrating only when they insist on calling it stalking. **-432**

11. Have you ever been fired?
- Never. **+4**
- In one instance I was swept out with everyone else during budget cutbacks, although my work performance had not been criticized. **+2**
- Fired is such a strong word. I prefer to think of it as a permanent sabbatical **-23**
- or a mutual agreement to leave. **-32**
- Look, I didn't harm any of the hostages! **-90**

12. Why have you changed jobs so frequently?
- Rapid changes in my profession. **+4**
- I like to try new things. **-5**
- I've got a problem with commitment. **-19**

- I just go where the witness protection folks tell me to go! **-32**

**13.** Why did you leave your current job?
- I had outgrown what that position had to offer, and opportunities for moving up were being phased out. **+5**
- The people there asked too many questions. **-45**
- Guess you didn't read the paper . . . **-144**

**14.** What are your salary requirements?
- It should be comparable to the going rate for someone in my field with my expertise. **+3**
- I don't know. How much are you pulling in? **-23**

**15.** How would you sell customers this stapler?
- Conduct lots of market research first. **+3**
- Make them an offer they couldn't refuse. **-32**
- Hire Girl Scouts. They sure move those cookies! **-95**

**16.** What are you currently reading?
- Some very informative books on innovative management, as well as the classics—you know, Melville, Hemingway, Conrad. **+7**
- I just finished *Seven Habits of Highly Successful People.* **+2**
- Actually, I only got to the second habit. **-44**
- I guess I wasn't the target audience. **-53**

**17.** Would you be willing to relocate?
- That's certainly a possibility, if you are willing to accommodate my needs. **+4**
- Sure, but actually this chair is fine. **-12**
- Can you guarantee a new identity? **-32**
- Will it be cold there? **-45**
- Sure. Anywhere but Tucson. Warrants. You understand. **-55**

18. Does working extended hours, if deemed necessary for the job, pose a problem to you?
- I'm no stranger to working long hours. I find I get a lot done after the office empties at five. **+5**
- You mean, like, overtime? **-10**
- No, that's usually the best time to call my brother in Singapore. **-32**
- Working late? That's what the pills are for! **-98**

19. Have you ever had to work with a manager who was hard to get along with?
- Sometimes that can be part of the job, but I tend to get along well with others. **+5**
- Well, yes. But we won't be hearing from him for a long, long time. **-45**

20. How do you handle tension with your present boss?
- I find that regular communication, such as staff meetings, tends to diffuse any situation. **+6**
- We sleep together. **-55**

21. Show me you have a sense of humor.
- Well, even in the face of adversity, I always seem to find the humor of the situation, which tends to help me through tough times. **+13**
- I'm here, aren't I? **-45**
- Pull my finger. **-56**

22. Your resume shows a noticeable gap in the last few years. Why?
- I took three years off to help Rwandan refugees. Oh, and there was my volunteer work with the American Cancer Society. **+9**
- You ever see *Midnight Express*? **-34**

**23.** Why should I hire you?

- I have over ten years experience in plastics, and I'm confident my skills can help improve production. **+3**
- Because, deep down, you like me? **-55**
- C'mon, Dad! Don't make this so difficult! **-65**

**24.** Prove to me that your interests in our company are sincere.

- I'm here because I'm interested in not simply furthering my career, but making lives better. **+3**
- Is this where I'm supposed to offer you money? **-44**
- I'm the only one who can detonate this bomb. **-144**

---

### YOUR DUMB QUESTIONS—AND
### WHAT THEY WILL COST YOU

In a job interview, sometimes it pays to keep your big trap shut, especially if you're about to ask:

- Do I get my own office? **-2**
- Do I get a door for my office? **-3**
- And a door to your office? **-33**
- Do you guys have a cafeteria? **-2**
- What's your hot lunch? **-4**
- Do you include organic vegetarian wheat-free lactose-free textured soy protein on the menu? **-43**

- How do you resolve employee complaints? **-12**
- What's your feeling on the Second Amendment? **-54**

- Do you guys use computers? **-8**
- Are they compatible with Nintendo? **-55**
- Will anyone be monitoring my Internet activity? **-145**
- Will anyone be reading my e-mail? **-154**
- Where can I hook up my police scanner? **-200**

- Do you have a mentoring prog
- Can I have someone to mentor
- Would you be my mentor? **-4**
- Would you be my mommy? **-45**

- Where is the break room? **-4**
- It has a couch, right? **-65**
- Are there security cameras? **-74**

- How long is lunch? **-12**
- Is lunch included in the eight-hour day? **-13**
- How long are the "rest periods"? **-43**
- How about coffee breaks? **-23**
- Do we get time off during the day to run personal errands? **-46**
- because the methadone clinic closes at three. **-54**

- Do I get a company car? **-34**
- Is it a stick? I can only drive an automatic! **-43**

- Are workers required to sign out office supplies? **-33**
- You people really don't review the office phone bills . . . do you? **-33**
- Is there a 900-number block on my phone? **-37**
- Do you know that new receptionist on the third floor? **-45**

- Whom do I report to? **0**
- What's he like? **-4**
- Is he cute? **-40**
- Will he read me stories? **-98**

- What's the deal on expense accounts? **-10**
- Who sees my expense reports? **-12**

ow closely do you examine receipts? **-34**
Will you accept any from my last job? **-34**
- Can I expense a weekend in Aruba if my secretary goes? **-34**

- What's the difference between a personal day and a sick day? **-3**
- Which one applies to nervous breakdowns? **-5**
- Can I try out a cough on you? **-45**
- How many weeks of vacation do I get? **-4**
- Can I take the company car? **-19**
- How many kilos does the trunk hold? **-21**

- What's the male/female ratio in the office? **-6**
- Are office romances frowned upon? **-94**
- Don't you think we'd be more comfortable on the couch? **-74**

- Is there a dress code? **-8**
- because the kilt is a family tradition **-7**
- and my boys need fresh air, know what I mean? **-233**

- Is there room to move up? **0**
- Is there room for my cousin? **-45**
- Is there room for my home-theater system? **-200**

# 3 | YOUR PRIVATE HELL (OR WORKSPACE)

Chances are you spend almost as much of your life in your office as you do at home. Many experts believe this is because we cannot escape our incessant need to be productive. We know better: home life is even less of a thrill than watching women golf.

So it behooves you to make this small, confined space called your office as comfortable as possible—to ensure high productivity, good morale, and a clean, fresh pine scent. But remember: because the office can often be construed as an extension of your personality, what you have on the walls or on your desk can reflect positively or poorly on your character. The key strategy: use your surroundings to score points without appearing too "precious." What makes an office "precious"? Do you pride yourself on your candy dish?

## WHAT'S ON YOUR OFFICE WALLS:

- your college diploma **0**
- from a respectable college **+2**
- from a junior college **-5**
- from Columbia University **+4**
- Columbia School of Broadcasting **-15**
- it prepared you for saying, "Attention KMart shoppers" **-30**

- diplomas from Ivy League schools **+3**
- Ivy League M.D. **+6**
- your name isn't on any of them **-15**
- No prob. Your urologist will never miss them. **-158**

- Your degree from art school **+2**
- the art school you read about on the back of a matchbook cover **-12**
- it's next to your framed portrait of Binky **-43**

- your certificate of excellence from the Zig Ziglar School of Sales Secrets **-10**

- "Held at the Red Roof Inn, June 23, 1997" **-13**
- "Diploma also redeemable for continental breakfast in lobby" **-34**

- company awards **-2**
- your employee of the week certificate **-6**
- from seven years ago **-12**
- from another company **-32**

- pictures of your vacation **-2**
- a picture of you and your boyfriend snuggling and kissing on your ski vacation **-4**
- a picture of you and your boss kissing on your vacation **-12**
- the picture has been taped back together **-14**

- a photo of a famous celebrity **-3**
- you're with that celebrity **+1**
- it's you and Richard Simmons **-75**
- you're just as fat in the photo as you are now **-127**

- large inspirational posters **-10**
- featuring sunsets **-14**
- rainbows **-17**
- unicorns **-32**
- both **-43**
- and an uplifting message **-19**
- "Be yourself, but be your best self!" **-34**
- and you're not even a guidance counselor **-45**
- you're a prison guard **-132**

- picturesque photographs of unspoiled nature **-4**
- picturesque photographs of your bachelor party **-32**
- your face is obscured **+2**
- by your boxer shorts **-102**

## YOUR CALENDAR:

- features famous landmarks **+1**
- features bikini-clad babes **-5**
- holding power tools (courtesy of Black and Decker) **-10**
- features cuddly animals from the endangered species list **+2**
- also holding power tools (courtesy of Black and Decker) **-23**
- features a beautiful waterfall **-4**
- or footprints on a wet beach **-3**
- with a quotation from Thoreau **-3**
- Emerson **-3**
- Emerson, Lake, and Palmer **+32**
- Whitman **+3**
- Slim Whitman **-10**
- Alexander Hamilton **+2**
- George Hamilton **-4**
- Thomas Jefferson **+4**
- George Jefferson **-5**

### JAVA JOURNALISM

**(The Sayings on your coffee mug, and
what they will cost you.)**

- "Hang in there, baby!" **-4**
- with a cat hanging on from a tree limb **-13**
- "Carpe Diem!" **-6**
- and you don't know what it means **-7**
- or care **+2**
- "Follow your Dreams!" **-15**
- "Dare to Dream!" **-24**
- "Second Place, 1993 Charleston Race Walking Festival"
  **-30**
- "Is it Friday Yet?" **-34**

- "Even Superman Spent Most of His Time as Clark Kent!" **-187**
- The entire poem "If" by Rudyard Kipling. **-1200**
- "Help the Blind, Buy a Pencil" **-1232**
- It still has pencils in it. **-2111**

## DESK MEMENTOS:

- the candy dish **-2**
- filled with jelly beans **-4**
- filled with Pepcid AC **+2**
- filled with Prozac **-30**
- which is empty by noon **-45**

- a Zen garden **-10**
- an herb garden **-44**
- a bonsai tree **-12**
- a shoe tree **-44**
- those metal balls that strike each other endlessly **-34**
- empty Coke bottles **-10**
- empty Jim Beam bottles **-52**

- paper clips **0**
- lots of paper clips **-3**
- which are fashioned into roach clips **-21**

- a small primitive wooden statue **-1**
- you claim it's a memento from your vacation in Jamaica **+2**
- we all know it's a bong **-33**
- not that we mind **+4**

- a paperweight **+1**
- a half-eaten tuna fish sandwich **-4**
- which you use as a paperweight **-19**

## WHAT YOU READ (OR PRETEND TO READ) AT WORK

- your mail **+4**
- other people's mail **-45**
- anything by Norman Mailer **-55**
- your local paper **-2**
- the horoscope column in your local paper **-23**
- the *Wall Street Journal* **+4**
- your own personal journal **-4**
- *Fortune* **+2**
- *Soldier of Fortune* **-45**
- reputable business books **+1**
- books by Tony Robbins **-10**
- books by Tony Danza **-33**
- that book on the seven habits of highly successful people (hint: one of them won't be "reads self-help book at work") **-41**
- anything with "chicken soup" in the title **-50**
- books on how to start your own business **-54**
- books on how to start your own cult (see Tony Robbins) **-300**

## YOUR COMPUTER

- You have an automatic back-up for your hard drive. **+1**
- You've got the fastest modem available. **+1**
- You've got your own scanner, as well as the latest in software. **+1**
- You still do nothing at work all day but play Quake II. **-14**

- You've got a real-time video card **+3**
- so you can create innovative, exciting presentations **+9**

- so you can watch Pamela Anderson and Tommy Lee's wedding/honeymoon video **-23**
- You only watch the wedding part. **-40**

- You've got a really cute novelty mouse pad. **-4**
- You've got a really funny screen saver. **-5**
- You've got a really "artistic" screen saver **-12**
- Edward Munch's *The Scream*. **-20**
- Your screen saver rivals your coffee mug for stupid sayings **-33**
- "Working hard or hardly working!" **-43**
- You've incorporated annoying cartoon sound effects into your software. **-13**
- You still can't save a file **-24**
- but that's what tech support is for. **-33**

## OFFICE DECOR

- You've got an ergonomic chair. **-2**
- You've got an ergonomic keyboard. **-5**
- You've got an ergonomic secretary. **+5**
- You've got an ergonomic groove in your desktop for the heels of your ergonomic shoes. **-23**

- You have rustic knickknacks in your office **-3**
- you refer to it as "bric-a-brac" **-20**
- and assorted bric-a-brac **-4**
- driftwood art **-5**
- spin art **-7**
- "kids with those really big eyes" art **-95**
- shrunken heads **-12**
- of former coworkers. **-543**

- You've got golf trophies **-3**
- bowling trophies **-7**

- hunting trophies **-12**
- you hang your raincoat on the antlers. **-33**

- You keep sports equipment in your office, to use at lunch **+2**
- running shoes **+1**
- bowling shoes **-4**
- snowshoes **-13**
- lawn aerating shoes **-33**

- a Frisbee to toss at lunch **+1**
- a hackey sack to kick around **-24**
- a crossbow to fire at small pets **-43**

- a baseball mitt **+1**
- an oven mitt **-44**

- a pull-up bar **+2**
- a monkey bar **-27**
- a minibar **+23**

- hiking boots **+2**
- riding boots **-3**
- bridle and saddle **-12**
- and you don't ride horses **-34**
- but you certainly have an intriguing nightlife **+10**

## OFFICE POLITICS

- You ask your boss for better office space **0**
- because you need more privacy to concentrate on your job **+3**
- You make beaded seat covers. **-30**
- The office will be closer to your boss, allowing better access **+4**
- and a better view **+2**
- of the adult drive-in across the street. **-34**
- More importantly, the window can be opened. **+3**
- You don't have to go outside to get high anymore. **-31**

- Your office is messy and unorganized. **-3**
- You jot down important information on any handy scrap of paper. **-6**
- You wrote your business plan on the tag for your laundry. **-10**
- You waste hours digging around trying to find it **-15**
- while the guy at the dry-cleaners is following up on your marketing and sales strategy **-23**
- and beats your quota by 45 percent. **-56**

- When people come into your extremely messy office, you're quick to defend yourself **-3**
- "A messy desk is the sign of a busy mind!" **-4**
- "I know how it looks, but I also know where everything is!" **-4**
- "See, there's the guacamole!" **-23**

- Even though your office is messy, you always find something the moment your boss comes in and asks for it. **+2**
- "Yep, here it is right here on my desk—last week's Beijing sales projections!" **+4**
- He sees it's from 1987. **-54**
- You point out that *is* last week according to the Chinese Zodiac calendar. **-65**

- You refer to your tiny cubicle as an "office." **-3**
- You like to call your cramped cubicle your "workspace." **-7**
- You actually have a nickname for your office **-10**
- "the Cave" **-11**
- "the Coolbicle." **-20**
- Everyone else has a nickname for your office, too **+4**
- the mail room. **-44**

- You tell all of your friends about your spacious corner office. **-10**

- They decide to visit you at work. **-13**
- You point out that, technically, the PhotoMat booth is all corner office. **-32**

- You sit in your boss's big corner office while he's at lunch. **-3**
- You send out dirty e-mails from his account. **-23**
- You peruse porno websites using his password. **-44**
- You hope that hot woman from market research will notice you sitting in this important office. **+2**
- She does. **+5**
- She's the key witness at your sexual harassment trial. **-43**

# WELCOME ABOARD!

It's your first week on the job. You're fresh, eager, and dying to make an impression (that could explain the musical number). Here's the score when you're the new guy or gal:

- When a fellow employee asks, you tell him about your previous job. **+1**
- "It was fine, but it didn't offer the excitement and opportunity of this place." **+2**
- "I'd rather not get into it, thank you." **-5**
- "Working odd jobs. Here and there. Nothing to tell really." **-33**
- "The less you know, the better." **-45**
- "I could tell you." **+2**
- "But then I'd have to kill you." **-14**
- Your coworkers admire your hip, dark sense of humor **+5**
- until you kill them. **-2800**

- During those first weeks on the job, you treat everyone with respect **+2**
- and listen more than talk. **+3**
- Rather than quietly learn the ropes, you give your opinion on major projects **-12**
- without knowing much about them. **-18**
- You suggest scrapping the five-year plan. **-19**
- You add that the company logo sucks **-22**
- and the mission statement is the dumbest thing you've ever heard. **-44**
- You work for the federal government. **0**
- "We the people, we the schmeople . . ." **-321**

<br>

- When people question your strong opinions, you simply say, "Well, this is how we used to do it at my old job." **-23**
- You were self-employed. **-34**
- You were a Macarena instructor. **-54**
- You actually worked for a high profile company **+5**
- as a safety consultant. **+8**
- You'd give out the name **-4**
- but you figure Value Jet got enough press. **-500**

<br>

- You spend the first month on the job criticizing how things are done. **-4**
- You preface each comment with, "Back at my old job, we did it differently." **-10**
- At the Medieval Times dinner theater **-45**
- you were a jousting knight. **-32**
- You insist on still wearing the chain mail. **-53**

<br>

- When you start a new job, you treat your coworkers with courtesy and respect. **+5**
- You presume an excessive level of familiarity. **-10**
- During the first meeting, you sit yourself at the head of the table **-12**

- and place your humidor to your left. **-19**
- You make up a nickname for your boss. **-22**
- You call him "Red" because he has red hair. **-43**
- You call him "Bubba" because he's from Arkansas. **-54**
- You call him "Tattoo" because he's short. **-76**
- You call him "Stevie" because of his guide dog. **-430**

- You learn your job quickly and efficiently **+2**
- and blend in well with the staff. **+9**
- So much so no one knows you're there **-3**
- which is just the way you like it. **-5**
- Then it's just you and the petty cash drawer **-44**
- and the tunnel you're digging to the cafeteria. **-123**

- It takes a lot of time for you to settle in. **-5**
- It's been a month, and you still haven't even learned the most basic duties. **-15**
- You keep trying to answer the fax machine. **-20**
- You think it's the mother ship **-45**
- wondering where you've been. **-100**

- You're quick to comprehend the dynamics of office politics. **+2**
- You know who to butter up in order to advance your career. **+1**
- You distance yourself from those who are clearly on their way out. **-3**
- Besides, you can still see Dad on weekends. **-45**

## MEETING WITH THE PERSONNEL DEPARTMENT

As a new employee, it's always nice to sit down with those friendly folks at human resources to discuss harassment policies, the generous 401(k) plan, day care, as well as whether you'll get a parking space for your Vespa. Of course, you'll have more important questions to cover.

- How many personal days do I get? **0**
- Can I trade them in for cash? **-23**
- Can I trade them in for food? **-40**

- What about sick days? **0**
- Do they cover hangovers? **-43**
- Do they cover hurt feelings? **-30**

- Do health benefits include eye exams? **0**
- Liposuction? **-12**
- What do you think these love handles will cost me? **-32**
- Do you have a prescription plan? **0**
- Does it cover medical marijuana? **-43**
- Do the benefits cover detox programs? **-54**
- Swedish massage? **-56**
- palm reading? **-63**

- Where are the smoking lounges? **-12**
- There won't be any drug testing, will there? **-43**
- What if I just wear long-sleeve shirts? **-54**

- Do you have a sexual harassment policy? **0**
- Yes? Mmm . . . guess that means tonight is out of the question . . . **-54**

---

- If I get injured on the job, will disability cover most of my paycheck? **-30**
- It will? **0**
- Aahhh! Paper cut! **-45**

---

# 5 | YOUR VOCATION

So you've got a job. Big deal. Now you've got to work on your personality. After all, each occupation comes with its own unique set of idiosyncrasies that differentiate you from the rest of your cohorts (if you're a manager, start working on that twitch). Do you fit the bill? Let's find out.

### You're an Administrative Assistant

- You get upset when called a secretary or receptionist **-3**
- but you cry when you don't get flowers on Secretary's Day. **-13**
- You're a proud official Mary Kay distributor. **-5**
- You've even got the pink Cadillac! **-9**
- You're great at wrapping gifts and picking out greeting cards. **+2**
- You know every maître d' in town **+4**
- though you've never eaten at their restaurants. **-4**
- You know more about your boss's personal life than your own **-5**
- because you pore over his expense reports. **-4**

- You really believe that "massage" was for his bad back. **-4**
- You have an overabundance of personal pictures on your desk. **-4**
- Your desk looks like the missing persons bulletin board at the police station. **-11**
- You've been thinking about getting a realtor's license. **-11**
- Once a month, you bring in your cat. **-11**
- You're simultaneously overprotective and terrified of your boss **-6**
- but the attraction is undeniable. **-8**
- You celebrate all the major holidays **-9**
- and even some of the minor ones **-23**
- decorative eggs for Easter **+1**
- a plastic tree for Christmas **+1**
- you come dressed as a pilgrim on Thanksgiving **-4**
- and in your groundhog outfit for Groundhog Day **-15**
- you put on your cheerleading outfit for the Rose Bowl **+10**
- you light candles for the anniversary of Princess Diana's death **-43**
- You have the best candy dish, and know it. **-8**
- You remember that we borrowed your office supplies **-4**
- and sulk until we return them. **-8**
- Now you label everything **-11**
- including the labeler. **-33**
- You complain about making copies for the boss **-3**
- and setting up appointments and reserving meeting space. **-6**
- You find such mindless work demeaning **-15**
- but when asked to do something intellectually challenging, you balk. **-21**
- "That's not in my job description." **-33**

## YOU'RE THE CAFETERIA LADY

- Your name is Madge. **0**
- You call the rest of us sweetie **-2**

- or shweetie, depending on how late in the day it is. **-6**
- Your hands are always wet. **-3**
- You've got a hearty smoker's cough **-3**
- which complements your hearty smoker's breath. **-4**
- When the crowd clears out, your boyfriend eats for free. **-4**
- You only seem to wipe your nose when you're serving food. **-12**
- You refuse to wear a hair net **-14**
- which adds a sense of adventure to the salad bar. **-17**
- You always wear cheap black sneakers and smoke Menthol Light 100's. **-4**
- You're saving your Marlboro miles for the cooler with built-in wheels. **-12**
- If we get on your good side, you let us slide on coffee. **+2**
- If we get on your bad side, you serve us the "funny" meat. **-10**
- You wear a Brooks and Dunn concert shirt under your apron. **-13**
- It covers the tattoo of a Brooks and Dunn concert shirt. **-14**

## You're the Computer Help Desk Guy

- You prefer that we call you an "analyst." **-3**
- We don't. **-5**
- You drink Pepsi before 9 AM. **-3**
- You wear a black T-shirt **-2**
- with "Byte Me" across the chest. **-4**
- If you weren't working on computers, you'd be working in a comic book store **-4**
- or hanging around James Doohan's grave. **-10**
- You could—but don't—read our e-mail. **-4**
- You named your pet ferrets Point and Click. **-13**
- Like computers, you must avoid direct sunlight. **-12**
- The guy at the drive-thru knows you by your beat-up Opal **-10**
- and the really cool "The Truth Is Out There" bumper sticker. **-12**

- Every answer somehow always ends in "dot-com." **-19**
- You take special delight in recounting the glitches you discovered in Windows 95. **-10**
- You judge the rest of us by our lack of RAM. **-12**
- Your come-on line: "So, what's your model number?" **-14**

## You're a Salesman

- You prefer to be called "account executive." **-5**
- You have breath mints in every pocket **-4**
- and you still smell like Jim Beam. **-8**
- Shake your hand, and we get a free business card! **-7**
- You ask for it back if we can't further your career. **-44**
- You try to hit at least one AA meeting a month. **-8**
- It's great for networking. **-10**
- You quote from the jacket flaps of books by sales gurus. **-17**
- You haven't read a whole book since college, so why start now? **-19**
- You have the "I'm not like other salesmen, I'm human" rap down cold. **-12**
- It helped you nail your coworker's wife when he was out on a call. **-123**
- You know the DUI tests by heart ("Z, Y, X, W, V, U. . . . ."). **-23**
- You cynically refer to a presentation as a "dog and pony show" **-10**
- but word has it you have a thing for both. **-61**
- You can calculate your commission down to the penny **-8**
- but can't figure out a tip without that laminated card. **-13**
- You've got a car trunk full of samples. **-5**
- You give them as gifts around the holidays **-30**
- and you're a pharmaceutical salesman. **-46**
- Everyone loved the Viagra **+12**
- but the folks who got insulin felt cheated. **-134**
- You've got a thick roll of bills in your pocket **-10**
- but $15 in your checking account. **-20**

- You're the life of the party when drunk **-2**
- but turn bitter and resentful at the end. **-23**
- The first thing you do on a business trip is take off the wedding ring **-30**
- the second thing: scan the phone book for old girlfriends **-32**
- the third thing: give up and order porn from Spectrevision. **-34**

### You're the Maintenance Guy

- You think desks are for sissies. **-4**
- You threw out our computers **-6**
- because you thought they fell off something. **-19**
- You always have a bottle, somewhere. **-19**
- You never worked out in your life **-3**
- but can kick our well-toned asses. **-20**
- You don't vote **-3**
- but you know who really killed JFK. **-12**
- You won't jump start our car **-14**
- unless, of course, it was made in America. **-14**
- You never follow politics **-3**
- except when those commie liberal pinkos in Washington want to take our guns away. **-30**
- You get a six-pack for what we pay for a single beer. **-3**
- You don't appreciate it when we recap *Seinfeld* episodes in front of you. **-8**
- Your key chain weighs more than our heads. **-10**
- You think pro wrestling is real **-13**
- but that Elvis faked his death. **-20**
- You believe any guy who drinks tea is a commie **-2**
- in that case, however, we're inclined to agree. **+4**
- You call in sick when Truckasaurus comes to town. **-8**
- You've got a belt buckle the shape of a Colt Revolver. **-7**
- You have at least one tattoo **-4**
- or at least one tattoo you tried to remove by yourself. **-33**
- You still call us "college boy" **-14**

- and we're in our fifties. **-34**
- You haven't seen a movie since they stopped making *Cannonball Run* sequels. **-12**
- You can fix everything with your pocket knife **+10**
- including bad relationships. **-78**
- You can smell our fear when you approach us. **-20**
- You can work through a heart attack. **-53**

## THE MALE SECRETARY

- You are a male secretary **-10**
- and you're not gay. **-55**
- You are a male secretary, and you don't let it get to you **+3**
- even though you're the only guy who holds that job in the company. **-4**
- Well, except for Joe **+2**
- and that's only because he hasn't had the operation yet. **-45**
- Yet you take pride in your position. **+1**
- You lunch with other secretaries **-1**
- and gossip. **-4**
- You really start to care about Charlie on "Party of Five." **-7**
- You go out with the secretaries after work **-5**
- and drink banana daiquiris **-6**
- instead of beer. **-9**
- You've taken to giggling after just one drink. **-32**
- You still get upset that Kathie Lee Gifford let Frank off easy. **-43**
- You can throw together a Longenberger basket in a heartbeat. **-45**
- You no longer notice—or mind—when the boss greets all the secretaries with, "Morning girls!" **-54**

## You're the Attractive Intern

- You hang high school or college formal pictures in your cubicle. **-4**
- You spend the first two weeks cowering **-9**
- and rearranging your formal pictures. **-11**
- You know the value of regular reapplication of lip gloss. **+3**
- You mistakenly think we would like to meet your boyfriend. **-10**
- You think we'll let you "follow us around for a day." **-10**
- But you'd report us if we followed you around for a day. **-20**
- You've seen *Jerry Maguire* three times. **-4**
- You're well-scrubbed and smell really good. **+4**
- You don't know you are the primary subject of sexual fantasy for all the married men in the office. **+3**
- You do know you are the primary subject of sexual fantasy for all the married men in the office **-5**
- which is why you're a restless sleeper the night before Casual Friday. **-6**
- You tell Mom not to call you at work. **-4**
- You look up to the administrative assistant **-8**
- because she's a whiz at those copier settings. **-10**
- You're frustrated over the meaningless work you do **-3**
- but spend an entire week writing a four-sentence memo. **-8**
- You honestly believe this internship might lead to a job offer. **-23**

## You're the Creative Type

- You think you're smarter than everyone else. **-4**
- You keep a copy of Proust in plain view **-9**
- next to your underground zines. **-12**
- You despise us because we once pulled your ponytail. **-13**
- You sing "No Woman No Cry" to impress us with your third-world sensibilities. **-13**

- You would appreciate it if we didn't borrow your CDs **-14**
- and then use them as coasters. **-9**
- You read the *Utne Reader* **-11**
- sometimes out loud. **-23**
- You wear black **-12**
- even in an August heat wave. **-19**
- You have a *New Yorker* cartoon tacked to your bulletin board **-12**
- next to your Amnesty International bumper sticker. **-23**
- You finally got your ear pierced **-9**
- that'll show the suits! **-23**
- You really, *really* want to go to Prague. **-12**
- Every week you try to grow a goatee **-20**
- and you always give up by Friday. **-30**
- You use chopsticks at lunch to show you can relate to foreign cultures **-10**
- even when you're having a burrito **-23**
- a vegetarian burrito. **-33**
- You're working on a novel **-15**
- it's "the first part of a trilogy" **-21**
- you're dying to tell us all about it. **-34**
- You find gender identification to be too constraining **-6**
- and you still can't get a date from either sex. **-33**
- You take the day off for Lollapalooza. **-34**
- You bought a four-wheel drive sport utility vehicle so you can "rough it" on weekends **-14**
- but you still can't change a tire. **-21**
- To show off your wild side, you want to get a tattoo on your thirtieth birthday **-34**
- but you chicken out **-38**
- and decide to grow that goatee again instead. **-40**
- You totally identified with Michael's crisis on *Thirtysomething*. **-12**
- You thought Elliot's wardrobe was really hip. **-45**

- You like to rail against the capitalist system **-23**
- in your $85 black Armani T-shirt. **-43**
- You like to boast of your affiliations to Greenpeace and the World Wildlife Fund. **-34**
- You'd prefer to keep it quiet when you land the Union Carbide account. **-43**

### You're the Outside
### Consultant/Management Trainer

- You insist that everyone fill up the front rows. **-14**
- You're proud of your handshake **-12**
- which you learned in a one-day handshaking seminar. **-21**
- Your hobby is winning over negative people. **-22**
- You often encourage us to introduce ourselves to the person sitting next to us. **-32**
- You like to say there's no such thing as a dumb question. **-34**
- You're prone to shout, "We are all Michelangelos!" **-40**
- as well as, "There are no bad ideas!" **-44**
- You like to quote Pat Riley **-13**
- but you found out later he coaches basketball. **-32**
- Many of your clients are in the Fortune 500 **+4**
- at least they used to be **-43**
- before they hired you. **-54**
- You never break your smile **-30**
- even when we try to run you down in the parking lot. **-45**
- No one ever sees you go to the bathroom (which should tell us something). **-34**
- You get paid two grand a day for going over the stuff in the big blue binder **+21**
- and if we skip ahead, you scold us. **-43**
- When people ask how you became a consultant, you tell them you decided to impart your years of experience to others. **-4**
- We all know you got fired from your last real job **-23**

- and that you're one step ahead of bankruptcy. **-44**
- Your letterhead has your office address as "Suite 8B." **-4**
- Everyone knows it's your apartment. **-34**
- You carry your own laser pointer **-70**
- it's monogrammed. **-98**
- You'd die if you found out where we've been sticking it. **-104**
- The $300 Ferragamo brief case matches your full-length sable coat. **-10**
- You're 46 years old and have no crow's feet **-20**
- because we paid for your plastic surgery. **-30**
- You really think we're kidding when we refer to you as a parasite. **-23**

# OFFICE ROMANCE

It's no surprise most of us find romance at work. Can you blame us? After all, that's where most of us spend most of our time (aside from detox). But there are risks whenever we become romantically involved with a fellow employee—and we aren't just referring to the rug burns (though that can be a problem).

- You have a reputation at work as being a principled employee who doesn't date coworkers **+3**
- because you believe it causes too much strife among the staff **+5**
- and creates potential for serious legal hassles **+4**
- what with your herpes. **-4**
- You just couldn't handle the rejection **-10**
- and besides, the house is in your spouse's name. **-20**

- Before you engage in any office romance, you evaluate the potential risks to your career and its advancement. **+3**
- You realize career advancement is highly overrated. **-24**
- After all, what good is a corner office with a couch and a wet bar if you don't have someone to share it with? **-122**

- You frequent meetings on sexual harassment policy **+4**
- wearing a towel. **-44**
- You go to these meetings because you believe it's helpful to keep up to date on the latest guidelines. **+3**
- Plus, it always helps to keep an eye out for any new loopholes. **-34**
- "They never said anything about the cafeteria help." **-44**
- You're hoping the hypothetical examples are graphic. **-17**
- You're always the first to volunteer to act them out. **-49**

- You always volunteer to run office tours to any new employee who wants them. **+3**
- Your boss admires your initiative. **+3**
- But she wonders why none of the ugly women know where the supply closet is. **-45**

- You treat coworkers of the opposite sex as professional equals. **+3**
- You insist on equal pay for equal work **+4**
- "and all that crap." **-4**
- Yet you still act like a gentleman, holding doors and offering to carry heavy packages. **+3**
- The women in the office respect you and consider you non-threatening **+4**
- as they drive off with that "dangerous" guy from the sales department. **-23**

- You are careful to maintain strict boundaries between your professional and personal life **+4**

- meaning, nobody at work ever meets your spouse -34
- meaning, nobody at work knows you're actually married. -45
- If they did, you'd have to break up with your assistant -84
- or at least break off the engagement. -132

- When a young, attractive employee flirts with you, you ignore it +3
- and change the subject. +5
- You add that you're married, too. +3
- When the employee says, "This will be our little secret," you pause. -4
- You've always been a fan of trust-building exercises. -45
- It's not cheating if it's not with a woman, right? -98

### THE OFFICE BREAKUP

- When it's time to break off the romance with a coworker, you do so responsibly +2
- so as not to cause any strain on the work environment. +3

- You break it off at a place far from work. +1
- You break it off in the parking lot, after work -7
- in the conference room, in your department -23
- during the weekly staff meeting -56
- "Kyle, since you can't get your sales figures up, we're going to have to cancel this merger." -23
- "Fine with me, Rachel. Considering it would be your fourth merger this week." -34
- "Loser!" -100
- "Slut!" -100

- You engage in a relationship with a coworker **-5**
- but it's okay because you're available and single, and so is she. **+3**
- Still, you suggest that it might be wise to keep your relationship under wraps **+4**
- because you realize it can put a strain on other coworkers **+5**
- and ruin your chances with the hot new sales manager. **-26**

- You are currently involved with an underling at work. **-4**
- You don't let it interfere with your professional objectivity. **+3**
- Within three months, you've promoted the employee to executive status. **-15**
- You send a memo praising her talents **-18**
- and her personal hygiene. **-25**
- "And she can cook, too!" **-45**

- You are romantically involved with a coworker, but you hide it well from your other coworkers. **+3**
- Whenever you and your lover leave together for hours at a time, you tell coworkers you're going to grab lunch. **-1**
- Still, everyone knows what you were up to. **-9**
- Because you never leave the parking lot **-22**
- or wipe the footprints off the inside of your windshield. **-29**

- You only display amorous affection on company turf when the place is completely empty **+1**
- like late at night, on weekends **-1**
- and absolutely only when you know it's safe. **+2**
- Then you've been known to make passionate love on the lobby floor **-5**
- and on the collating table. **-8**
- You delight in keeping this little secret from everyone else. **0**
- Until the security camera video becomes a big hit at the Christmas party. **-89**

## BE CAREFUL WHOM YOU SLEEP WITH. . . .

Your choice will cost you points, as well your reputation. Here's what you lose when you sleep with:

- a single, available coworker **0**
- a single, available coworker with a friend in the legal department **-46**
- a subordinate **-6**
- an ambitious subordinate **-10**
- an ambitious subordinate who is good with electronic surveillance equipment **-78**
- the UPS delivery person **0**
- the Fed Ex delivery person **0**
- the mailman from the post office. **-76**
- the "disgruntled" mailman from the post office. **-125**
- the groundskeeper **-10**
- the groundskeeper with the gun collection **-30**
- the mail room guy in the Whitesnake T-shirt **-12**
- who's never been the same since 'Nam **-13**
- the fix-it guy who replaces the light bulbs **-13**
- and lives in a trailer on the property **-25**
- He wants to show you his underground play room. **-245**
- the copier repairman **-345***
- the intern **-40**
- the interns **-80**
- the intern who thinks you really do love her **-144**
- and has your poems to prove it **-187**
- actually, the special prosecutor has them **-404**

*Why such a low score? Very hard to get toner off your blouse.

# IS IT SEXUAL HARASSMENT?

Monday you say "Hello." Tuesday you say "Nice weather." Wednesday you say "Nice blouse." Thursday you're sitting in human resources, explaining why back rubs really can boost team morale.

You should have known better.

- You have heard complaints from female coworkers about sexual harassment, and you decide to do something about it. **+4**
- You move the company to Texas **-12**
- where just about everything goes. **-30**
- You tell your secretary she doesn't have to bring you coffee anymore **+10**
- or at least in the French maid outfit **-23**
- but the fishnets have to stay. **-43**

- You hire a consultant to help come up with a sexual harassment policy for your company. **+4**
- You institute the policy immediately. **+4**
- You wait a few days **-9**
- at least until you can break it off with the consultant. **-12**

- At work, you are careful to use bias-free language. **+4**
- You always use gender-free pronouns and frown upon sexist banter. **+4**
- You treat women with the respect they deserve. **+5**
- They still won't go out with you **-14**
- because they're pretty sure you're gay **-21**
- which could explain all the Streisand CDs you got for Christmas. **-12**

- You work hard at incorporating bias-free language into your memos. **+10**

- You think He/She is that new guy from Taiwan. **-10**
- You call stewardesses "flight attendants." **+2**
- You call them when your wife leaves town. **-33**
- You refer to the new head of the board as the new "chairperson" **+3**
- "with the killer rack." **-90**

- You meet with a new rep hired to handle shipping for your company **0**
- over drinks. **0**
- You ask the rep, "Do you provide special services to big customers such as us?" **0**
- You wink when you say "special services." **-50**
- She gets offended. **-56**
- To calm her you say, "When I said 'special services' I meant discounts on extra large packages!" **+2**
- Then you add, "I hope you know what I mean by 'extra large packages.'" **-145**

### HOW TO TELL A DIRTY JOKE AT WORK AND NOT GET IN TROUBLE

#### The wrong way:

"So this guy walks into a bar and he sees these Siamese twin hookers sitting with a German shepherd . . ." **-30**

#### The right way:

"Excuse me, but I was just curious. Somebody just told me this joke, and it really upset me. I was wondering if it was sexual harassment. Let me get your opinion: So this guy walks into a bar and he sees these Siamese twin hookers . . ." **+2**

## HOW TO TELL A COWORKER SHE LOOKS NICE WITHOUT GETTING SUED

### The wrong way:

"Wow, Janice, you really look nice today." **-4**

### The right way:

"Because I am fully aware that words carry a wide range of meanings, and that many compliments, innocent though they may be, could be misconstrued as sexually charged in nature, when they really aren't, I'd just like my lawyer here (point to the guy in the suit carrying a leather briefcase) to inform you that—in no uncertain terms—you, Janice, um, look really nice (instruct lawyer to hand Janice copy of page 878 of Webster's Dictionary with the definition of nice highlighted)." **+12**

- You see a woman in the halls that you're attracted to, so you work up the nerve to ask her out for Friday night. **0**
- She says, "I'm sorry, I have to wash my hair." **-4**
- You ask her out again. **-7**
- She says, "No, I have to spackle my bathroom." **-10**
- You ask her out three more times. **-15**
- Finally she suggests a meeting place after work. **+2**
- The courthouse. **-40**
- You consider the restraining order her way of playing hard to get. **-45**

- You keep a comfortable distance from employees when you talk to them. **+3**

- Comfortable to you, however, is a high-school prom slow dance. **-12**
- You often touch employees when you talk to them **-6**
- on the shoulders **-2**
- upper back **-4**
- around the waist **-10**
- around the copier. **-33**
- You only touch women—never men. **-16**
- You only grope one woman in particular. **-20**
- When she asks you to stop, you apologize profusely. **0**
- You tell her you're just a "touchy-feely" kind of person. **-30**
- "I just can't help it—I'm Italian and we talk with our hands!" **-14**
- and your hands were saying . . .
- "Wow! You must use a Stairmaster!" **-32**
- "Are these Hanes?" **-54**
- "34C, definitely a 34C." **-65**

### YOUR SEXUAL HARASSMENT CHECKLIST

| Action | Verdict |
|---|---|
| a friendly wink | no |
| a lewd wink | maybe |
| followed by a lick of the lips | yes |
| a congratulatory hug in the hallway after she receives a promotion | no |
| with a kiss on the cheek | no |
| the hug lasts three minutes | close |
| so does the kiss | really close |
| your hands aren't visible | hey! |

| Action | Verdict |
| --- | --- |
| neither is your tongue | yes (if there are witnesses) |
| asking an employee out for drinks | no |
| repeatedly asking an employee out for drinks, after many refusals | not yet, but getting there |
| bringing a bottle to her apartment at 2 AM | it better be the good stuff |
| repeatedly asking an employee for back rubs during staff meetings | yes |
| repeatedly asking for less teeth | no, only natural |
| being reprimanded by a supervisor for hitting on employees | not a good sign |
| hitting on the supervisor after you've been reprimanded | yes, but we admire your gumption |
| you tell a female employee her dress really brings out her eyes | no, that's a nice gesture |
| you tell a female employee her dress really brings out *your* eyes | yes |
| you ask a coworker to dinner to show your appreciation for her good work | no |
| you ask a coworker home to show her your new waterbed | trick question (no one has waterbeds anymore!) |
| a gentle pat on the shoulder | no |
| on the lower back | no, but getting close |
| on the behind | bingo! |

| Action | Verdict |
| --- | --- |
| you claim it was an accident | all right, we'll cut you a break |
| you meant to touch her breasts | get a lawyer |
| you talk about your sex life in public | yes, it creates a hostile environment |
| you offer to show your homemade videos | yes (unless the offer is accepted) |
| you leave flowers on a coworker's desk as a congratulatory gesture over a promotion | no, that's a nice thought |
| those flowers come with a room key | yes |
| and the room has a vibrating bed | nice touch |
| calling anyone "honey," "sweetie," or "darling" | yes (unless you're an adorable old codger) |
| calling anyone "babycakes" from a payphone at 3 AM | yes (especially if you're an adorable codger) |
| saying, "You look nice." | no, but be careful |
| saying, "You look hot." | yes |
| saying, "You look hot, what with this humidity." | nice save! |
| "Nice tie." | perfectly safe |
| "Nice blouse." | translation: nice breasts, so yes |

# CRASS COMMUNICATION

In the work environment, there is potential for trouble every time you open your mouth (especially if you rarely floss). Here's how your point tallies can rise and fall based on your communication skills.

- You keep your complaints to yourself. **+3**
- You tend to whine a lot **-3**
- especially about your boss. **-3**
- "He's always barking orders at me." **-5**
- "Everyday he's got me walking a tightrope." **-4**
- "He has me jumping through hoops." **-4**
- "He's got me running around in circles, and juggling five things at once." **-5**
- "It's like a three-ring circus!" **-6**
- It is a three-ring circus. **-8**
- "How come I always go on after the elephants?" **-12**

- You often use cliches to get your workers moving. **-4**
- "Noses to the grindstone, people!" **-4**
- You make grindstones. **-44**
- "Kick ass and take names!" **-5**
- You run a day care center. **-64**
- "It's the bottom of the ninth, boys." **-4**
- You're a hockey coach. **-22**
- "This isn't rocket science!" **-13**
- You make ICBMs. **-23**

- You show respect for the older employee who works for you by calling him "sir." **+1**
- You address him as "Old man." **-5**
- You address him as "Driftwood." **-14**

- You yell "Dead man walking" when he passes you in the hall. **-45**
- You grease his cane. **-200**

- Even though you're white, you attempt to "street talk" when you see a black employee in the hall. **-9**
- " 'S'up bro?" **-7**
- "Hey, man, word up!" **-9**
- "Yo, look who's in the house!" **-12**
- "That memo was, like, whack!" **-34**
- When he brings his family by, you say, "This must be your posse!" **-87**
- Yet you always flinch when he reaches up to adjust his glasses. **-100**
- You took it as a compliment when he said your last report was "bad." **0**
- It wasn't meant to be. **-112**
- When you said he looked "phat," he decked you. **-123**

- You like to pepper your work conversation with phrases you picked up serving in the armed forces. **-4**
- When hard work has to be done, you talk about "going to war." **-8**
- When someone puts something in your in-box, you scream, "Fire in the hole!" **-15**
- When something unsavory must be done, you say, "Jump on that grenade!" **-20**
- You refer to the bathroom as "the poop deck." **-30**

# BUILD YOUR OWN BUZZ WORDS!

Why rely on tired old jargon and stupid catch phrases when you can make up some of your own? The next time you need to impress (or thoroughly confuse) a client or coworker, give these fabricated fragments a try:

| Jargon | What It Means |
| --- | --- |
| an after-school special | a particularly cute college intern |
| photocopier | a worker-bee intern |
| Pontiac Sunbird | an intern you can beat on all day like a rental car |
| man, he killed a lot of ducks | a major screw up, like the Exxon Valdez |
| uncoupling | removing your wedding ring when traveling on business |
| Joe works for Wang | Joe's boss is a prick |
| management material | spineless incompetent |
| great people skills | completely lacking in practical talent |
| going global | so inebriated you have the spins |
| he's P.O.O. (pronounced: poo) | shit-canned, as in "pursuing other opportunities" |
| grandfathering | falling asleep, then drooling, in a meeting |
| idea chairman | someone who is incapable of doing any real work (see great people skills) |

| Jargon | What It Means |
| --- | --- |
| *take a trip to Mars* | leaving the meeting to get something from the candy machine (then never coming back) |
| *pull a C-Span* | go ahead and leave early, no one's watching |
| *an Ikea dresser* | a shaky deal that's probably going to fall apart in a month |
| *Can you direct me to the appliance department?* | what's with the short sleeves and tie? |
| *I believe that's New Coke* | don't worry, he'll be gone in a month |
| *Four Seasons and a driver* | the company's expensing the whole trip |
| *Cheeto* | A guy back from a "business trip" so tan he's orange |
| *brought to you by Monsanto* | a boring presentation |
| *pulling a Walt Disney* | the CEO who will neither die nor retire |
| *cab fare to Calcutta* | disguising an outrageous expense on your travel sheet |
| *kitty litter* | an employee you can pretty much shit all over |
| *brown-bagging* | dating the UPS guy |
| *the women's movement* | secretaries who must get their coffee in groups |

| Jargon | What It Means |
|---|---|
| *pulling a Rosa Parks* | upgrading from coach to first class |
| *a sit-up* | what you do when the old man walks by |
| *screwing the pooch* | having sex with a dog |

## THE WONDERFUL WORLD OF STUPID CLICHES

Sometimes it's not what you say but how you say it, that scores. . .

1. What to say when you want to sound too busy to do any real work:
- "I've got a lot on my plate right now." **+2**
- "I've got too many irons in the fire." **+3**
- "I've got a lot of pigs in my blanket." **-33**

2. What to say when it appears you aren't doing any work on a vital project:
- "I'm just letting the ideas *marinate*." **+3**
- "Right now it's on the *back burner*." **+3**
- "I'm letting it *stew*." **+4**
- You're a short-order cook. **-22**

3. What to say when you want to avoid accepting more work:
- "I'd love to, but I've got to *run it by* someone." **+3**
- That someone is your mother. **-20**
- She says it's okay, as long as you clean your office first. **-32**

4. What to say when you want to blow off someone:
- "Let's *touch base* next week!" **+1**
- You're on vacation next week. **-2**

- *"Call my people,* we'll set something up." **+4**
- You don't have any people. **-2**
- Well, except for the Village People. **-34**
- You used to be the construction worker. **-40**

5· What to say when your boss asks you a question and you weren't listening:
- "Mm . . . sounds like a *can of worms* to me." **+2**
- "Mmm . . . sounds like a *can of Fresca* to me." **-4**
- "Frankly boss, *that dog won't hunt.*" **+4**
- "Frankly boss, *that gerbil won't nestle.*" **-9**
- "I see a big *red flag,* chief." **+4**
- The boss is showing you a big blue flag. **-34**

6· What to say when you're too scared to choose between two or three competing ideas:
- "I say we *throw them against the wall and see which one sticks.*" **+4**
- You work for Pampers. **-23**

# DID YOU GET MY MEMO?

Memos are God's gift to the corporate coward. They allow you to discredit another employee without ever getting near him. But remember: whatever you put down on paper remains there forever. Think of that the next time you send a Xerox copy of your privates to the CEO and tell him to "Downsize this."

- You don't spend too much time writing memos. **+3**
- You keep them relevant and concise. **+4**
- "Screw you, Jackson." **-23**
- You write long memos **-8**
- which take an entire day to write. **-10**
- You need to find that perfect quote from Thoreau to start it off right **-15**
- and that precious cartoon from the *New Yorker.* **-34**
- It's folding it into an origami swan that takes so much time. **-44**

- You keep your memos to the point **+3**
- which you learned in a seminar on business writing. **+3**
- Sometimes you go too far, and forget the simple courtesies. **-3**
- "Johnson has been promoted to regional manager." **-4**
- "The current regional manager, Sobel, is history." **-35**

- In a memo you play up your role regarding recently completed projects **-4**
- even though you had little to do with their success. **-14**
- "I'm happy to report Bill did some great field research *under my supervision.*" **-16**
- "Janet came up with a brilliant cost-benefit analysis. It was a pleasure *guiding her every step of the way.*" **-23**
- "Arthur ably demonstrated a well-designed plan at the sales conference." **+4**
- "You may have noticed I let him use my pointer." **-54**

- When you write memos to the staff, you lighten them up with touches of humor. **+2**
- You insert a joke or a cartoon **+2**
- but only if it is relevant to the topic. **+3**
- Sometimes you make up a memo just to circulate a joke. **-3**
- "It looks like we've got our budget well in hand." **+4**
- "Speaking of 'well in hand,' George Michael walks into a men's room . . ." **-15**

- The point of your memo is to break some bad news to employees. **-4**
- The bad news: major layoffs. **-9**
- You try to accentuate the positive while presenting this harsh reality. **+3**
- "I can happily report that we have found a way to solve our parking problem." **-50**
- "For those of you wishing to spend more time with your kids—we've got great news!" **-52**
- "Now all of you in customer service can catch up on your soaps!" **-54**

 

- You always read over all of your memos before sending them. **+2**
- You never send out a memo you wrote while angry. **+2**
- You shelve it until your temper cools. **+4**
- You have to bribe the mail room guy to retrieve a memo **-10**
- the one you fired off to the company president **-18**
- the one that says, "Our love is greater than any cost-containment strategy!" **-245**

 

- To make yourself look important, you "cc" people who really don't need to read the memo **-4**
- the company president, the chief financial officer, the chairman of the board. **-16**
- You hope everyone will see the list and think you're a real up-and-comer. **-30**
- Instead, you get a memo back from the president **+5**
- to tell you he's firing you **-100**
- to save on paper costs. **-233**

# 10 | MEETINGS

Meetings offer endless opportunities for looking important, impressing the boss, and burning up a few hours with pleasurable nonproductive banter. But it's also a chance to make a complete fool of yourself. For example:

- When a meeting is going on longer than you planned, you stay and endure it. **+3**
- You get up and leave. **-3**
- You employ your "fake cough" **-1**
- the one you use at every meeting. **-12**
- Your boss transfers you to the Riyadh office, where the desert air will be good for your lungs. **-34**

- You flash a signal to your assistant outside the conference room. **0**
- She pulls you out for "an urgent phone call." **+3**
- She pulls the fire alarm. **-20**
- She pulls your tongue **-23**
- during your fake epileptic seizure. **-34**

- During meetings, you listen intently to what the boss and other coworkers have to say **+1**
- and take careful notes throughout **+1**
- and make sure everyone sees you taking notes **-34**
- You actually find yourself fantasizing about all sorts of things **-6**
- like sleeping with all of the Spice Girls **-5**
- in a really cool-looking spacecraft. **-10**
- When your boss asks you a question you fail to respond. **-12**

- When your boss repeats the question, you say, "Well, Maria, that's an excellent question" **+3**
- "but I don't think we've resolved Tom's earlier question." **+3**
- Tom didn't have a question. **-10**
- Tom doesn't work there anymore. **-23**
- Tom's been dead since July. **-54**

- Your boss asks you a question during a meeting. **+1**
- You weren't listening. **-4**
- You stare at him blankly. **-20**
- You say, "Oh, I'm sorry. I was just thinking of a way of streamlining our production process that will probably save us millions of dollars." **+6**
- Your boss asks you what it is. **0**
- "I'll put it on paper for you." **+3**
- You draw him a really cool-looking spacecraft. **-45**

- When you're in a meeting, you occasionally volunteer for projects if no one else is willing to do the job. **+3**
- Actually, you make a point to volunteer for everything, constantly raising your hand and shouting, "Oh! Oh! Oh!" **-9**
- Coworkers start calling you Horshack. **-23**

- You arrive at a meeting with a pen or pencil, a legal pad, an appointment book, and a calendar **+4**
- which gives everyone the impression you're well-prepared and genuinely interested **+4**
- or it certainly would have **-3**
- if you hadn't shown up at the wrong conference room **-13**
- on the wrong day **-30**
- in the wrong town **-45**
- and the locals find a new "pocket" for your laser pointer. **-103**

- During meetings, you encourage employees to bring up ideas during the discussion. **+2**
- You offer encouragement even when the ideas don't click. **+3**

- When ideas are brought up, you don
- which suggests the ideas don't even me.
- You say, "I'm sorry, you must have confuse. bad-ideas' meeting." **-23**
- You say, "You don't plan on putting down roo. you?" **-30**
- You proudly unfurl your cat-o-nine tails. **-32**
- You pull out a revolver and say, "Ever see *The Deer Hunter*?" **-398**

- You contribute key ideas and themes during weekly meetings. **+4**
- You make a point to stay awake during meetings. **+1**
- Still, you often find yourself nodding off. **-3**
- You bring your favorite blanket **-15**
- it matches your bunny slippers. **-40**

## DUMB THINGS YOU SHOULDN'T DO AT MEETINGS

- being obvious about sitting next to the boss **-8**
- being obvious about agreeing with everything he says **-12**
- even when he says, "You're sitting too close to me" **-33**
- being funnier than your boss **-11**
- being funny at the expense of your boss **-32**
- staring at employees longer than appropriate **-6**
- trying to send them coded messages with eye blinks. **-23**
- having "second thoughts" about something you've known about for 3 months **-4**
- like your 3-month plan **-14**
- letting us "hear what's on your mind" **-7**
- it's the theme song to *The Facts of Life* **-44**
- verbally attacking a colleague **-5**
- ridiculing a colleague on a personal level **-9**

- trying to tear off his disguise while shouting, "He's a spy!" **-40**
- simply trying to make a point **+1**
- with logic **+2**
- with a letter opener **-40**
- for the sake of argument, playing devil's advocate **-9**
- taking it literally, and slaughtering a chicken as an offering **-244**
- being dramatic, like getting up and walking around behind us while talking **-5**
- then pummeling someone with a baseball bat **-45**
- dozing at the table **-5**
- snoring at the table **-9**
- banging your head on the table **-12**
- mumbling incoherently in your sleep **-23**
- and making more sense than when you're conscious **-27**
- volunteering for any project **-5**
- volunteering someone else for a project **-6**
- who isn't at the meeting **-12**
- and doesn't even know where Indonesia is **-34**
- or how to operate a land-mine detector **-132**

# 11 | SPEECHES AND PRESENTATIONS

Ask anyone what they fear most, and you might expect to hear something like "death," "plane crashes," or "a french kiss from Joan Collins." But no, the most feared event in our lives is public speaking. With good reason. The risk of screwing up and losing points is vast. And the opportunities for gaining points, sadly, are few. Why? Because nobody remembers a decent speech, but they never forget a horrible one. Just ask Reggie White.

- To help hone your speech, you practice your remarks in front of the mirror at home the night before. **+4**
- You practice making the speech in front of a few close friends and family. **+3**
- They heckle you. **-12**

- You join Toastmasters in order to hone your public speaking skills. **+3**
- You join Toastmasters because you think it will involve a lot of drinking. **-14**
- You're the only person to bring a bottle. **+5**

- Before making a presentation, you try to get some background information on the person introducing you. **+1**
- "Thanks, Dick, for that kind introduction, and thanks for the great job on the renovation of the downtown marina." **+6**
- "Thanks, Dick, for that kind introduction, and so sorry to hear about your wife." **-33**
- "But I guess some women don't realize their true sexual orientation until later in life." **-98**

## AUDIOVISUAL AIDS

### Major presentation? Here's how you score, gadgetwise, if you use:

- a large video screen, which you control from a laptop **+4**
- full color charts **+3**
- movie clips to drive home a point creatively **+3**
- from *Rocky* **+2**
- from *Patton* **+3**
- from *Behind the Green Door* **-43**
- flowchart **+1**
- flip charts **+2**
- Flip Wilson **-4**
- overhead projector **-4**
- overhead projectiles **-40**
- flashlight pointer **+1**
- flash cards **-4**
- flash dancing **-12**
- dry wit **+6**
- dry ice **-33**
- dry martinis **+12**
- a water gun **-5**
- a flare gun **-130**
- a nail gun **-200**
- bar graphs **+3**
- skin grafts **-40**
- Steffi Graf **+14**

- You come to a large auditorium filled with people, prepared to give a twenty-minute speech. **+2**
- You find out you are slotted for one hour. **-5**

- You slow down the pace of your speech so it will last the entire sixty minutes **+2**
- by doing your own simultaneous Spanish translation. **-15**
- When you finish, you still have thirty minutes left. **-4**
- You decide to recap the points you made. **+2**
- You decide to open up the time for questions. **+4**
- Nobody has any. **-9**
- Well, actually there is one question. **+5**
- "You call that a speech?" **-15**
- "Are there any more donuts?" **-30**
- "When does the presentation start?" **-45**
- "Can we go home now?" **-54**

- After the presentation, you're asked a question **0**
- which you answer with confidence. **+3**
- You don't know the answer to the question **-5**
- so you say, "That's a great question, but since Bob works in that area, perhaps he would like to field that one." **+2**
- You turn to Bob. **0**
- Bob is snoring. **-32**
- Bob is missing. **-45**
- Bob was asking the question. **-65**
- You can't answer the question, so you attempt to end the exchange by saying, "I think it's time we allowed some questions from the other side of the room." **+3**
- The other side is empty **-12**
- except for the guy with the vacuum cleaner. **-20**

- To add excitement to your presentation at the sales conference, you decide to make a video. **+3**
- You use the latest audio and visual effects to make this sales video shine. **+9**
- You slip it into the wrong box **-10**
- and return it to Hollywood Video. **-13**

- The sales reps are treated to a special viewing of *Bag Ladies in Bondage*. **-87**
- They proceed to have their best quarter in ten years. **+45**

- To calm your nerves while making a presentation, you employ a number of stress-reduction techniques you've learned over the years. **+3**
- You imagine yourself on a quiet tropical beach. **+4**
- You chant a simple phrase over and over again to "center" yourself. **+2**
- "Must relax, must relax, must relax . . . " **+3**
- "Must not screw up, must not screw up, must not screw up . . ." **-13**
- Try saying it silently to yourself next time. **-50**

- You try to liven up the duller parts of your presentation, like the financial projections. **+4**
- You come dressed as Nostradamus. **-13**
- You come dressed as Jimmy the Greek. **-33**
- You come dressed as Jeanne Dixon. **-40**
- During the question-and-answer period, you refer to your Magic 8-Ball. **-54**

- You try to involve the audience and make your speech "interactive" by directly addressing members of the group. **+3**
- "What do you think is the number-one issue facing our industry today?" **+4**
- "How would you define a progressive workforce?" **+4**
- "Is this thing on?" (followed by tapping the microphone) **-4**
- "Which one of you is snoring?" **-9**
- "Hey, that nearly hit me!" **-23**

- You try to end your presentation on an up note. **+3**
- You end your presentation with a poem. **-4**
- You end your presentation with Zeppelin lyrics. **-8**

- "If there's a bustle in your hedgerow . . . " **-12**
- You thank everyone for listening. **+3**
- You tell everyone you enjoyed speaking to them. **+3**
- You end your speech with, "Peace." **-5**
- You end your speech with, "Party on." **-20**
- You ask everyone to hug the person next to them. **-39**
- You organize a line dance. **-54**


- You try to warm up the crowd like a comedian would **-1**
- or a talk-show host. **-9**
- You start off by asking the audience, "ARE WE HAVING FUN YET?" **-15**
- "I CAN'T HEAR YOU!" **-30**
- "HELLLOOOO!" **-45**
- "OKAY PEOPLE! ONE MORE TIME . . . ARE WE HAVING FUN YET?" **-40**
- "THAT'S MORE LIKE IT! YES!" **-55**
- "NOW THIS SIDE OF THE ROOM!" **-76**
- "NOW THE OTHER SIDE!" **-78**
- "TOGETHER!" **-80**
- "OKAY! EVERYONE FIND A PARTNER." **-198**
- "HEY, WHERE IS EVERYONE GOING?" **-321**
- "PUT THAT GUN DOWN!" **-432**

- When you do your slide-show presentation, you try to keep it interesting. **+2**
- You think it's clever to spell out everything on your slides **-20**
- and capitalize! **-23**
- "So what's the answer? I-N-N-O-V-A-T-I-O-N!" **-20**
- "How do we grow? D-E-C-E-N-T-R-A-L-I-Z-E!" **-40**
- "Why am I here? H-U-G-E S-P-E-A-K-I-N-G F-E-E!" **-50**

# 12 | EXTRACURRICULAR ACTIVITIES

No, we aren't talking about sex with tipsy clients. This is far more important stuff: the post-work activities that seem disarmingly casual, but still offer major opportunities for profound humiliation. Whether it's the company picnic or the department softball team, you're still being scrutinized, which means, of course, leaving the air rifle (and your strange cousins) at home.

## THE COMPANY PICNIC

- At the company picnic, you come dressed casually but properly attired. **+2**
- You wear clean, pressed khakis and a neat polo shirt. **+3**
- You come dressed in whatever you normally wear when you aren't at work. **-4**
- like those Lycra shorts **-5**
- those really snug Lycra shorts **-9**
- or the leather jacket **-12**
- and the leather chaps **-40**
- and the leather corset. **-54**
- You deliberately lose the sack race in hopes that you'll be "punished." **-50**

- You wear your favorite cut-offs **-9**
- with the rips you added yourself. **-12**
- They clash with your bright red half-shirt. **-32**
- And you're over forty **-14**
- and over forty pounds overweight. **-50**

- You're wearing a T-shirt **-15**
- with a lurid saying emblazoned on it **-8**

- "If there's grass on the field, play ball!" **-15**
- "Lock up your daughters." **-18**
- You work for the Girl Scouts of America **-76**
- in charge of recruitment. **-248**

- You use the picnic to meet higher executives that you normally don't have the opportunity to approach. **+2**
- You introduce yourself to all of them. **+2**
- You pat them all on the back. **+1**
- After eating a plate of baby-back ribs. **-10**
- You talk with them on topics that interest them **+4**
- like their various hobbies and recreations. **+2**
- "How's that boat of yours, Mr. Simpson?" **+2**
- "Been fishing lately, Mr. Cooper?" **+2**
- "How's that lawsuit going, Mr. Murphy?" **-4**
- "Gee, they sure looked like women in the newspaper photos." **-32**

- You impress the muckety-mucks by showing how serious you are about your job. **+2**
- You talk about work while you're there. **-8**
- You bring work with you to the picnic. **-10**
- You offer to fax the results of the egg and spoon race to the satellite offices. **-32**

- You participate in many picnic games. **+2**
- You decide to take part in the sack race **+3**
- because you've been training. **-13**
- You suggest to your assistant that perhaps "we should double up." **-44**
- You go bobbing for apples. **+2**
- You go bobbing for interns. **-54**
- You decide to take part in the "three-legged race" **+3**
- which you win easily. **+4**
- which you graphically misinterpret **-198**

- You refrain from drinking too much at the beer truck. **+3**
- After a while, you start drinking a lot. **-4**
- You start acting "wild and crazy." **-8**
- You think it's time you show everyone "the real you." **-10**
- You crash the talent show and sing "Louie Louie." **-12**
- You can't remember the words. **-30**
- You worry later that you may have soiled your reputation. **-43**
- You fail to notice that you soiled your pants. **-113**

## THE COMPANY SOFTBALL TEAM

- You play on the company softball team **+1**
- and you organize the practices. **+1**
- You ensure a sense of fun by not taking the recreation too seriously. **+2**
- You institute your own version of "spring training." **-4**
- You institute fines for missing practices. **-9**
- You post "cuts" in the company newsletter. **-21**
- You institute a cup check **-30**
- at work **-34**
- with a bat. **-45**

- You go out for the team because you're just out to have a good time. **+2**
- It's an excuse not to go home right after work. **-3**
- It's an excuse to drink beer outside instead of in your garage. **-4**
- You don't even play **-6**
- you just ring the bell for the beer inning **-11**
- which is every inning. **-19**
- You spend all of the game hogging the beer cooler. **-21**
- You tell everyone you're "carbo loading." **-24**
- It's the "carbo unloading" in the dugout that's ticking everyone off. **-49**

- You're the one guy on the team who takes the game too seriously **-9**
- because you're an ex-jock who used to play **-10**
- because you never played organized sports **-11**
- and now you finally have your chance. **-12**
- You actually stretch. **-13**
- You heckle **-11**
- and swear **-14**
- and berate players on your own team **-19**
- including the guy with the stump. **-121**
- You wear a cup **-14**
- and make a point of adjusting it (just like the pros). **-16**
- You bring your own bat **-19**
- with pine tar. **-24**
- You oil your glove during your lunch hour. **-34**
- You've named your glove. **-38**
- "Glovey." **-39**
- You wear spikes. **-40**
- You've named them, too. **-44**
- You slide into home **-34**
- when the play isn't close **-45**
- flattening the catcher. **-50**
- That sixty-year-old receptionist never saw it coming **-87**
- neither did her new hip. **-200**

## WHAT'S YOUR POSITION? WHAT DOES IT MEAN?

| | |
|---|---|
| first base | you're fat and slow, but you're also the department head |
| second base | you suck, but the coach works for you and wants a raise |
| shortstop | you're the only player who remembered to bring the beer |
| third base | smart: you're close to the dugout, which means you're closest to the beer |
| right field | you sign the expense sheets (which explains the uniforms), so they had to put you somewhere |
| center field | you work in the mail room part time, but no one else can run more than fifteen yards without clutching their chest |
| left field | you're the only player who sees well enough to catch a fly ball |
| pitcher | you can't reach the plate, but, hey—you're the president! |
| catcher | you're the smart one: you can ask opposing batters about job openings at their company |

# 13 | THE SCORECARD FOR SATAN (UH, WE MEAN MANAGERS)

Managers may be the most hated creatures on this wonderful blue orb we call Earth. And for good reason. They not only make our lives difficult by issuing vague orders and then reprimanding us when we follow them, they also use strange phrases like "feedback," "cost containment," and worse, "kudos." Is it any wonder that 87 percent of all inmates currently on death row were once mid-level managers? It's true. We read it in *Forbes*.

## THE PROGRESSIVE MANAGER

- You are compassionate when it comes to an employee's personal problems. **+3**
- You express heartfelt sympathy when a relative passes away. **+7**
- You pull the bereaved aside and say touchingly, *"Whatever you need."* **+9**
- Then add, "That's the slogan for our new sports drink! What do you think?" **-23**

- When a relative passes away, you offer the employee extra time off. **+4**
- You tell the employee to "Take as much time as you need." **+12**
- When she returns, you introduce her to her replacement, Clara. **-23**
- Who happens to be a very old woman. **-23**
- You explain, "Clara's relatives are already dead." **-70**

- You're the type of boss who tries not to be a boss in the traditional sense. **+2**
- You're the type of boss *you* always wanted to have. **+3**
- You give your employees flex time to suit their lifestyle. **+4**
- You let them dress casually, and take off early when the weather is nice. **+5**
- You give them extra personal days if they've used up all their allotted days. **+5**

- which is why all your employees love you **+10**
- until you fire them for being 45 percent off budget. **-65**

- A good employee asks for a richly deserved raise. **0**
- You don't want to lose a valuable employee, but you just don't have the money. **-4**
- So you offer him perks and benefits instead **+2**
- a company car, extra vacation time, a much larger office. **+3**
- You offer him flexible hours. **+2**
- You offer him a flexible chair. **-4**
- You offer him a Flexible Flyer. **-44**
- You offer him a brand new title. **+2**
- And a laminated gold nameplate to go with that title! **-17**
- Vice-President for Procurement. **+3**
- His first procurement assignment: Nameplates! **-45**

- When an employee asks for a raise, you come up with new ways to say no. **-5**
- "When you ask for a raise, it sounds like you're asking for more responsibility." **-4**
- "So why don't we jot down everything you think you can do in the next twelve months—and next year we'll see if you earned that raise!" **-15**
- You help her come up with a list of goals. **-6**
- Many of them are vague. **-12**
- "Goal One: Evaluate core competence to its fullest extent." **-20**
- "Goal Two: Augment goal one by evaluating a prototype." **-30**
- "Goal Three: Streamline process from goal one to goal two." **-40**
- "Then compare and contrast." **-45**
- She says these goals don't make any sense. **-50**
- You ask her to put that in writing. **-75**

- After years of hard work, you finally make it to the upper echelon of the corporate hierarchy. **+2**

- You are stunned to find that the "old boys' network" is still in place. **0**
- Frankly, you're disgusted by this kind of behavior **+4**
- until you take part in it. **-5**
- Then, you admit, it is kind of fun. **-8**
- delegating all the difficult projects **-11**
- handing out lucrative contracts to friends and family **-20**
- talking incessantly about golf **-21**
- smoking big cigars **-26**
- talking about the breast size of female employees. **-34**
- It *almost* makes you wish you were a man. **-203**

 

- You pride yourself on your decisiveness **+5**
- although sometimes you're not sure. **-13**
- You make your decisions based on cool reasoning and sober analysis. **+5**
- You seek out the opinions of others when making decisions. **+3**
- You consult an advisory board. **+2**
- You consult a Ouija board **-33**
- a dart board **-35**
- and you're the most successful stockbroker in New York. **+34**

 

- You think of yourself as a progressive manager. **-5**
- You strive to make the work environment more inviting. **+1**
- You add organic, flavored coffees and all-natural low-fat snacks to the snack bar. **+1**
- You replace bagels with rice cakes. **-20**
- You pipe in soft, new age music. **-1**
- You force people on hold to listen to Yanni. **-178**
- You make every day Casual Friday **+3**
- so you can show off all your caftans. **-33**
- You help reduce stress by replacing the fluorescent lighting with soft natural lighting. **+1**

- You help prevent back pain and wrist disorders by ordering comfy ergonomic chairs. **+3**
- Now everyone naps **-22**
- which helps relieve their eye strain **-10**
- from all the soft lighting. **-22**

- You set a relaxed, casual example for your staff. **+4**
- You start wearing sandals **-25**
- and loose, vaguely Tibetan or Ecuadoran clothing **-30**
- which always gets stuck in the door of your new $85,000 Mercedes SL4. **-65**
- You start the day off with morning meditations. **-33**
- You quote famous mystic gurus. **-24**
- You cull management advice from books by Deepak Chopra **-87**
- as well as fashion tips. **-100**
- You encourage an honest, open exchange of emotions **+3**
- meaning you lose your temper at the drop of a hat **-45**
- only now you call it "cleansing the soul." **-46**
- Your "talking stick" has a nail on the end of it. **-65**

- You hire a consultant to teach your staff stress-relieving exercises they can do right at their desks. **+2**
- They relax their shoulders by doing neck shrugs four times a day. **+3**
- They strengthen their forearms by doing "paper scrunching" exercises **+3**
- using their requests for pay raises. **-15**
- They tone their glut muscles by performing butt crunches in their chairs. **+5**
- Your department calls itself "The Hardbodies." **+4**
- Management calls them "Dead Weight." **-34**

- You encourage employees to expand their earning potential by taking continuing education courses. **+3**

- You push them to get that extra degree and learn a second language **+4**
- and brush up on their accounting skills **+5**
- and develop sophisticated programming expertise **+10**
- until you realize that tuition fees have tapped out your budget. **-20**
- You fire them all. **-35**
- "Sorry, it just seems like you're all overqualified." **-67**


- You often form committees to analyze problems. **-5**
- The committees rarely meet, however. **-10**
- They're all waiting for the report from your Joint Study Group on Problem-solving Techniques. **-20**
- This week's topic: Meeting refreshments—seltzer or spring water? **-45**


- When you're about to ask an employee to do something unpleasant you don't beat around the bush. **+1**
- You tend to joke around **-2**
- and make small talk before getting to the point. **-4**
- "So, any big plans for the weekend?" **-5**


- You like to "incentivize" your employees. **+3**
- You actually use the word "incentivize" in conversation. **-4**
- You offer bonuses and awards that go beyond salary. **+14**
- You offer cold, hard cash. **+20**
- You offer "positive reinforcement." **-7**
- Other people call it "spanking." **-80**
- You give out Employee-of-the-Month awards. **-11**
- Everyone is an Employee of the Month. **-21**
- You affix gold stars to outstanding memos and reports. **-10**
- You give fruit baskets **-4**
- or an inspirational plaque **-33**
- that reads "Great Work, Fred." **-33**
- Even though his name is Robert. **-45**

- Actually, her name is Mary Ellen. **-84**
- You tell her a real team player would change her name to Fred. **-121**

- You're always willing to make new employees feel welcome. **+4**
- You show them where to get office supplies **+2**
- from other people's desk drawers. **-4**
- You show them how to acquire office furniture. **+2**
- You give them directions to Goodwill **-32**
- as well as what to do about any other problems. **+5**
- Meaning, you show them where you hide the bottle. **-44**
- You carefully describe their duties and responsibilities **+6**
- perhaps you're a little vague **-10**
- "Oh you'll find out soon enough." **-15**
- and then ask if they can operate a wood chipper **-100**
- at night. **-200**

- You encourage employees to suggest improvements. **+3**
- You've got an "idea box" in your office. **+4**
- It looks just like your out-box. **-6**
- It looks remarkably like your garbage can. **-10**

- You arrange a meeting to discuss an employee's lagging performance. **+4**
- You ask if there are problems at home. **+3**
- There are. **0**
- You sympathize. **+3**
- You give him the free time so he can deal with these problems. **+4**
- The "free time" comes with the lousy severance package. **-35**

- You explain assignments clearly and precisely **+4**
- including the results you expect. **+2**
- You instill enthusiasm by pointing out the positive aspects of the project. **+3**

- "It's a great way to get to know the technical staff." **+2**
- "It's a great way to get to know the cleaning staff." **-1**
- "Since you'll be seeing them every night around 11:00 PM." **-21**

- You allow employees a sense of control over each new assignment. **+4**
- "I trust you to set your priorities as you see fit." **+4**
- "You may need to log some overtime." **-2**
- "Or try to fit it in with your regular work." **-3**
- "Like Feldman does." **-3**
- "Or Feldman *did*." **-9**
- "You *remember* Feldman, don't you?" **-19**

- You try to mediate conflicts between employees. **+4**
- You meet with the employees individually. **+2**
- You then bring both employees together to reach a compromise. **+2**
- You mediate the conflict using a progressive "conflict-resolution" tool. **-3**
- You learned that in a management training course last year. **-8**
- You hand them pillows **-12**
- you hand them Nerf baseball bats **-14**
- you hand them Thai fighting sticks. **-45**
- You tell them this is how "we" did it in Burma. **-213**

- You resolve conflicts between employees swiftly **+3**
- unless it's between two women. **-5**
- Then you do your best to egg it on. **-15**
- You'll seize on any opportunity to yell, "Cat fight!" **-34**

- You set up a plan to retain quality employees for the long term. **+5**
- You respect and reward experience and seniority. **+6**
- You heartlessly cut loose older employees. **-12**

- The phrase "But I carried you for nine months" just doesn't get to you anymore. **-36**

- When you are upset with the actions of an employee, you never express your dissatisfaction in front of others. **+3**
- You always express your dissatisfaction in front of others **-3**
- so that the employee might serve as an example for others. **-3**
- The employee is humiliated. **-45**
- The employee is pilloried. **-75**
- The employee is flogged. **-321**
- The employee is forced to read management training manuals. **-1000**

---

### DUMB THINGS MANAGERS SAY AND DO

- "It's not in the budget" **-3**
- when referring to extra staff **-5**
- when referring to your raise **-6**
- when referring to your paycheck **-56**
- when referring to the handicap ramp **-87**
- at the hospital. **-432**

---

### THE MANAGEMENT TRAINING SEMINAR

- You go to a management training seminar **0**
- and do your best to participate. **+2**
- You engage in "trust-building exercises." **-2**
- You get excited when the facilitator says, "Now, I'm going to close my eyes and fall backward, and I have to trust you to catch me!" **-3**
- You yell, "Mine! Mine!" **-10**
- You say, "I thought *you* had him." **-47**
- The company docks your salary for the medevac helicopter. **-145**

- During the seminar, you are asked to play a game that tests your ability to make decisions and delegate. **0**
- The facilitator says, "You're in a lifeboat with six other people. You have limited provisions for only a few days. What would you do?" **0**
- You say, "Measure and distribute the food carefully" **+2**
- and "have survivors make fishing rods out of boat wreckage" **+3**
- You quietly fantasize what Ron—the fat guy from accounting—might look like glazed in butter. **-45**
- The facilitator calls you and another employee up to the front to engage in a role-playing exercise. **-3**
- The facilitator looks at you and says, "You're a manager who is having trouble dealing with this employee. How you would handle this?" **0**
- You hit the employee with a right cross. **-321**
- You turn to the employee and say, "I'm concerned about your work behavior. Is something distracting you from your work?" **+3**
- You add, "If that's the case, maybe we can work something out." **+3**
- Then you hit the employee with a right cross. **-423**

## MANAGING YOUR SECRETARY
## (SORRY, WE MEAN ADMINISTRATIVE
## ASSISTANT, OF COURSE!)

- Instead of calling your secretary a "secretary," you give the person a really nice title. +2
- associate staff assistant +3
- senior office manager +3
- executive coordinator +5
- you never use the title -5
- you just call her "mommy" instead. -13

- You have an assistant, and give him challenging duties that offer valuable experience. +4
- You hand him slopwork. -4
- You have him do your entire job -9
- including unseemly duties you don't want to do -23
- like firing employees -33
- like firing himself. -44
- "I think it's better if you hear it from you." -87

- You do not ask your assistant to run personal errands for you. +4
- After all, that's not what she's paid to do. +5
- You wait until after work before you ask. -14
- Then she's on her own time. -6
- "Remember, pantyliners with wings." -33

- You are sensitive to your assistant's desire to advance to a higher position. +6
- You encourage her to try new things +4
- and offer valuable advice. +7
- "Next time, wear a thong." -6

## THE HIRING SCORECARD

You decide to hire a job applicant because:
- She's talented. **+3**
- She knows your boss **-10**
- in the biblical sense. **-13**
- You used to date her **-15**
- and she held onto that last roll of film. **-30**

- You need a third baseman for the softball team **-29**
- and this guy looks like he's got a great arm **-30**
- and his dad owns a beer distributorship. **-35**

- He plays golf **-15**
- he doesn't play golf **-17**
- but he's willing to caddy. **-18**
- She's smart. **+2**
- She's cute **-19**
- she's really cute **-32**
- she's not cute, but your standards are low **-40**
- and so is the starting salary. **-14**

- He's got impressive credentials **+4**
- he's the only guy you interviewed **-19**
- he knew all the answers to your *X-Files* trivia quiz. **-56**
- You owe someone a favor **-44**
- meaning, you borrowed ten grand from his uncle **-50**
- who is in the "import/export" business **-54**
- and has a "Free John Gotti" bumper sticker on his Lincoln town car. **-65**

- He happens to share the same alma mater **-50**
- "Put it there, you fighting Penguin!" **-100**

- She's an old pal from college days **-24**
- and does she have stories! **-35**
- Not to mention your transcripts. **-60**

# 14 | RAISES AND PROMOTIONS

You work hard. You're never late. You still make barely enough money to cover your losses at the track. It's time to move up. Let's see how upwardly mobile you really are.

- When you ask for a promotion, you tell your boss exactly why you deserve this upward move. **+3**
- When you ask for a promotion, you desperately exaggerate your duties. **-4**
- You "helped the company streamline its environmental response program" **+3**
- meaning, you separated your trash into the right recycling bins. **-8**
- You "helped improve working conditions for the labor force" **+4**
- you started showering regularly. **-12**
- You "found new ways to improve morale" **+5**
- the basement vending machines now offer Twizzlers. **-9**
- You "helped institute the company's first job-share program" **+7**
- by getting everyone to do your work for you. **-23**

- You come prepared with a list of accomplishments to persuade your boss you deserve a raise. **+4**
- Since you've been playing third base, the company softball team hasn't lost a game. **-5**
- Since you've come aboard, the department has experienced one full year of jam-free copying! **-9**
- You point out no one has died on your watch. **-12**
- Well, except for Johnson **-134**
- but he had it coming. **-444**

- You point out the cops are happy with the kickbacks. **-34**
- And thanks to you, no one will be hearing from the health inspector for a while **-143**
- which leads you to another topic: the "mystery stew" you arranged for the cafeteria. **-400**

- When asking for a raise, you nobly downplay your personal achievements. **+4**
- You hope the success of the group will reflect on your leadership skills. **0**
- "You know, the credit goes to the entire staff—I couldn't have done anything without them." **+3**
- Your boss agrees with you. **-9**
- "And here I was thinking about giving you a promotion!" **-34**

- When your old coworkers drop by after you've been promoted, you say, "Great to see you." **+3**
- "Man, I miss you guys." **+4**
- "Um, do you have an appointment?" **-10**
- "Uh, how did you find me?" **-14**
- "Uh, do I know you?" **-22**
- "Security!" **-54**

- Now that you've been promoted, your demeanor does not change. **+2**
- You always were a prick. **-14**
- You still joke around with your old friends who now work under you. **+4**
- Even though you're their boss, you still drink beers and play golf with them on the weekends. **+5**
- You even find a way to have the company pick up the tab. **+10**
- "I found some extra money in the budget." **-11**
- They never saw the layoffs coming. **-240**

# 15 | THE ART OF FIRING, BEING FIRED, AND QUITTING TO RUN OFF AND JOIN THE CIRCUS

Every job must come to an end. Just make sure it's not your butt on the chopping block.

### When You're Wielding the Ax

- When firing an employee, you pull him into your office and talk to him privately. **+1**

- You explain in honest terms that his work just wasn't quite up to snuff **0**
- and you feel it's best for him to move on. **+2**
- You sit quietly and let him gather his thoughts **+3**
- as you hand him packing boxes. **-40**

- You prefer not to fire people face to face. **-12**
- You leave the bad news on voice mail. **-14**
- You send a memo. **-18**
- You send for security. **-60**
- You take an ad out in the paper **-4**
- advertising for his replacement **-12**
- and leave it on his desk. **-60**
- You casually introduce him to his replacement. **-23**
- It's a helper monkey. **-143**
- You invite the staff to a career-planning seminar but add, "Except you, Stevens." **-45**
- You ask for volunteers for next year's United Way drive, and when the hands are raised, you say, "Don't bother, Stevens." **-55**
- You ask him for his computer password, then transfer all his files. **-12**

- You suggest it may be premature for a young buck like him to settle down. **-14**
- He's in his fifties. **-34**
- You introduce him to "our new account executive" **-4**
- and there is only one account. **-12**
- You ask him if his wife is pregnant. **-3**
- When he says no, you say, "Good thing." **-14**
- You leave the classified ads on his desk with job openings circled in bright red ink. **-13**
- You tell him there's a package waiting for him at personnel. **-4**
- You don't mention it's a severance package. **-45**
- You offer him a transfer to a less lucrative territory. **-4**
- You tell him business is really picking up in Rwanda **-43**
- but you can't afford moving expenses. **-65**
- "But here, we got you this handy water purification kit!" **-76**

- When you do fire an employee, you soften the blow with a substantial severance package **+12**
- and by offering him a drink **+3**
- which, as it turns out, is his severance package. **-45**

- You offer to personally help the fired coworker find new work **+4**
- with some potentially fruitful job leads. **+7**
- You tell him you usually pay the neighborhood kid five bucks to mow your lawn. **-189**
- You slip him an extra buck for raking. **-211**

## Is *Your* Job in Jeopardy? Some Very Obvious Signs

- Your opinion no longer counts. **-9**
- The opinions of employees much younger than you are solicited instead. **-9**

- The random thoughts of the janitor carry more weight than yours **-53**
- and you know this. **-12**
- He's just taken over your accounts. **-284**
- And increased profits by 32 percent. **-612**

- You are handed less and less substantial projects. **-10**
- The stupid, meaningless projects don't even pass your desk. **-15**
- Interns are doing more important work than you are **-30**
- high-school interns **-38**
- including the one from "the special school." **-55**
- Your boss finally gives you a project **+3**
- with no set deadline **-12**
- and no real direction. **-14**
- You suspect he's given you busy work. **-33**
- Although you admit the Rolodexes move much more smoothly with laminated cards **-22**
- and the doorknobs smell lemony fresh! **-39**

---

### THE FASTEST WAY TO GET FIRED

- not fulfilling the basic requirements of your job **-13**
- not fulfilling the basic requirements of your job, and blaming it on "evil spirits" **-14**
- taking credit for other people's work, and getting caught **-4**
- taking credit for other people's work, without checking to see if their work was any good **-13**
- sexually harassing an employee **-45**
- sexually harassing an intern **-55**
- sexually harassing the fax machine **-494**
- causing embarrassment for the company at charity functions **-50**

- telling the kids at the Make A Wish Foundation to "get a life" **-76**
- stealing office supplies **-23**
- showing up on the security tape stealing office supplies **-60**
- showing up on the security tape trying to steal the security camera **-70**
- firing handguns in the bathroom **-100**
- not posting an e-mail notifying everyone that you would be firing handguns in the bathroom **-200**
- doing drugs before work **-124**
- doing drugs at work **-213**
- doing drugs at work, and you're not Robert Downey Jr. **-243**
- downloading pornography from your office PC **-83**
- from your boss's office **-98**
- sharing it with others **-49**
- charging for peeks **-54**
- charging unrealistic expenses on your company card **-30**
- like gifts for friends **-54**
- expensive clothes for yourself **-84**
- a Fabergé egg **-432**
- a bald eagle egg (you were hungry) **-543**
- sleeping on the job **-87**
- drinking on the job **-97**
- spilling a martini on the flight panel **-321**
- being a decent employee who goes about his or her work quietly **-334**

## QUITTING GRACEFULLY

- When you quit your job, you leave on good terms with everyone **+2**

- including your boss **+3**
- whom you didn't like very much. **+4**
- You realize it's smart not to burn any bridges. **+3**
- You don't let that stop you from stealing the client list **-19**
- or pilfering software of a purely proprietary nature **-20**
- or crashing the network by sending thousands of e-mails to Afghanistan **-30**
- as well as leaving an inflammatory message on your boss's voice mail. **-31**
- "Later, lard ass." **-33**
- "Dude, I'm like your hair—gone!" **-45**
- Then putting in an order for 75,000 Magic Markers **-49**
- and billing it to the cafeteria. **-55**
- stealing all the paper trays to the copiers **-32**
- replacing them with convincing replicas **+32**
- spiking the coffee with Ex-Lax **-40**
- spiking the coffee with angel dust **-928**
- Productivity jumps by 200 percent. **+40**

## THE JOYS OF UNEMPLOYMENT

Once you've been fired, you could fall into a deep depression, waste your hours watching educational television (instead of more important stuff like *When Animals Attack!*), and coming up with new ways to steal the neighbor's paper. Or, you could look at the bright side of things.

- You start working from home. **+5**
- After all, you've been told you have a terrific "phone voice." **-12**
- You see each day as a new beginning as you jump right out of bed! **+3**
- at 3:30 PM **-24**
- you were up all night counting bourbon bottles. **-68**

- You begin writing a corporate plan for your company +3
- "step one: explore demand for leftover pizza boxes in backyard." -87
- You tell yourself it's great not to have an office job because now you can wear whatever you want and no one will care! +3
- meaning bunny slippers—all day, every day -20
- at least you keep your bathrobe tied shut +3
- since the paperboy reported you -31
- again. -43

<br>

- You decide to spend your free time performing volunteer work in the community. +4
- You offer to serve soup at a homeless shelter. +4
- This makes you feel like you're making a real impact +5
- at least on your budget +6
- all those free meals are saving you cash. -4
- You spend your weekends picking up trash on the freeway. +5
- You like doing your part to keep the environment clean +5
- so does the judge who imposed the sentence. -33

## THE BURNOUT SCORECARD

It may be time to call it a day, if:
- The work you used to enjoy doing is no longer fun -2
- even when you try to make it fun. -8
- There's only so many pranks you can play manning the suicide hotline. -40

- You start overlooking the minor details of your job. -5
- You become careless with even those most basic of duties. -15

- You're an emergency room surgeon. **-56**
- "Right leg . . . left leg . . . it's all the same thing." **-98**

- Your temper is getting shorter **-10**
- you snap at employees and underlings **-12**
- you snap at clients. **-30**
- "Grow up, for Christ's sake!" **-90**
- You're a child psychologist. **-45**

- You yell at inanimate objects, like your computer **-5**
- you apologize to your computer for yelling **-8**
- you both enter counseling together **-100**
- you try to make it up by buying it roses. **-186**

# 16 | OFFICE PERKS

Some people see the phone, the computer, and all those neat pens and pencils as important tools to help you do your job. You know differently. It's an invisible economy, to be used and abused to make up for your lousy salary.

### THE PHONE

- You rarely use the phone for personal business. **+2**
- You call your significant other once a day. **0**
- You call your significant other numerous times throughout the day **-9**
- from other people's phones **-12**
- from your cubicle **-5**
- using the speakerphone **-32**

- using the emergency phone in the elevator. **-44**
- You try to call another elevator. **-88**

## OFFICE SUPPLIES

- You invite your boss and her husband over for dinner. **+8**
- You realize you haven't hidden all the stolen office supplies. **-34**
- You stuff everything in the closet **-10**
- and under the beds. **-13**
- The boss still recognizes your end tables **-44**
- which look remarkably like Canon laser jet copiers. **-345**

- You steal pens and pencils **-3**
- boxes of paper clips and yellow note pads **-4**
- computer disks **-8**
- expensive software **-12**
- really expensive hardware **-65**
- company cars **-234**
- copper piping off the building **-232**
- the boss's medication **-343**
- and now his hallucinations have returned. **-400**
- He actually thinks he sees you doing work. **+20**

## TRAVEL EXPENSES

- You don't abuse the perks that come with your job. **+4**
- But you do tend to go overboard on expenses. **-4**
- Accounting asks you why you had to fly first class instead of coach. **-4**
- You tell them your doctor says you need the leg room. **+2**
- You're only 5' 2". **-44**
- You are asked about the $150 spent on "market research." **-4**
- You show the receipt **+3**
- which reads: "milk 75¢, eggs $1.24, lightbulbs $3.70, Budweiser $5.43." **-10**

- You charge to the company six weeks of scuba classes, a wine-tasting course, and a seven-day spa vacation at an exotic resort. **-98**
- You write this all off as "self-improvement" **+2**
- which can only enhance "job productivity" **-12**
- then they see the bill for the plastic surgery. **-134**
- You needed to look good for your picture in the company newsletter. **-200**

When the accounting department calls you up about the $750 receipt for dinner at a sushi restaurant, you:

- tell them you were entertaining a large group of Japanese executives interested in importing the company's products. **+5**
- Your company specializes in big and tall clothing for men. **-20**
- You explain your idea for marketing them as tents. **-40**

## YOUR HEALTH PLAN

- You have a generous health benefits package, but you don't abuse it by running up doctor visits and tests. **+2**
- You treat the doctor's office like a bar—you've got your own seat and everyone knows your name. **-9**
- You fake workplace injuries to collect disability. **-23**
- "Copier-related post-traumatic stress syndrome." **-43**
- But you're still playing shortstop and batting clean-up for the company softball team **-45**
- and taking part in the company talent show **-50**
- with your trapeze act. **-210**

## THE CALLING CARD

- You never use your company calling card to make long distance personal calls **+2**
- unless you can't find your own card. **-4**

- You insist those calls are business related **-8**
- including those made to the Psychic Friends Network. **-14**
- "Market forecasting." **-33**
- And those calls to the "Coed Lust Line"? **-34**
- All part of your intern recruitment program. **-49**
- "Jiggling Judy" starts next week. **+10**

### HOTEL ROOM EXPENSES

- You never touch the minibar when traveling **+3**
- because everything is so expensive **0**
- and you're scared you'll get caught. **-5**
- You buy your snacks and soda elsewhere **+4**
- but help yourself to the little liquor bottles. **-12**
- You refill them with water so you don't have to pay. **+3**
- You still run up a big bill. **-12**
- It might have been that $45 can of macadamia nuts **-10**
- or the $54 bag of Famous Amos cookies **-12**
- and there was the bathrobe you stole **-30**
- and the ice bucket you pilfered **-12**
- and the damages you incurred for moving the mini-refrigerator into the bathtub. **-94**

## 17 | BUSINESS DINING, SCHMOOZING, AND OTHER TYPES OF TORTURE

Just because you're no longer in the office but at some high priced joint populated by waiters who write screenplays, don't think for a minute The Scorecard is suspended. You're still working, and you're still being watched. Score wisely, and you'll go far. Don't order Jell-O shots as an appetizer.

## DINING WITH CLIENTS

- When you invite a client out for lunch, you deftly slip your credit card to the waiter before your guest can protest. **+3**
- The waiter returns and hands it back **-4**
- and says you have exceeded the limit on your card. **-20**
- "Excellent!" you say. **+2**
- "I wanted to sue the credit card company but needed to be humiliated in front of a major client first." **+12**
- Your client digs into her pocket for her Mastercard. **-30**
- You apologize, and ask that this not undermine the credibility of your work **-10**
- as a budget consultant. **-40**
- You ask for a doggy bag for the dinner rolls **-55**
- which, as it turns out, is large enough to hold three place settings! **-100**

## ENTERTAINING A CLIENT

- You're entertaining a hip client, so you decide it might be cool to take him to something hip. **+2**
- You've got tickets to the Smashing Pumpkins **+4**
- make that backstage passes. **+7**
- To gear up, you spend the week trying to grow a goatee. **-7**
- The extra-strength Rogaine doesn't help. **-22**
- Neither does the Magic Marker. **-50**

- At the concert, you try to appear younger than you really are. **-3**
- You unbutton the top button of your Brooks Brothers shirt **-4**
- and put on your Killer Loops **-7**
- which clash with your Today's Man double-breasted suit. **-30**
- When you get inside, you try not to stand out **+2**
- even though you're the only guy carrying a briefcase **-11**

- and spring water -13
- and binoculars. -12
- Your cooler filled with finger sandwiches gets confiscated. -20
- The security guard tells you to lighten up on the watercress. -22

- You spend the entire concert trying to prove you're super cool. -4
- You convince your client the heart medication you're taking is actually Ecstasy. -23
- You chop up your Advil, and offer him a line. -33
- You dive into the mosh pit -34
- and ask everyone to stand still so you can retrieve your tie clip. -45

## SCHMOOZING

- When schmoozing clients over lunch, you try to establish a close relationship. +3
- You ask about the clients' background +5
- about their family +6
- about their alleged mob connections. -30
- You ask if that pinkie ring came with a finger. -58

- You share some personal information about yourself +2
- your interest in fishing +4
- your interest in fishnets. -15
- You remove your pants to show them your favorite pair. -34
- You don't brag about your health +2
- or go on and on about your heart rate +1
- cholesterol levels +1
- or percentage of body fat. +4
- Although you point out you're as regular as a Timex since you've been mainlining Mueslix. -44

- You don't complain about your declining health **+3**
- or the recent bypass operation **-4**
- or the double bypass. **-9**
- But you do show the scar. **-33**
- "See, it looks just like a zipper!" **-45**


- You never bring up your sex life. **+3**
- Actually, you like to talk about your sex life **-4**
- and, lately, what Viagra has done to it. **-45**


- You refrain from talking politics. **+3**
- You keep your feelings about nuclear power under wraps **+4**
- as well as your thoughts on gun control. **+5**
- You were too busy recounting your UFO abductions. **-40**


- During lunch, you try to impress the clients with your knowledge of the business world. **+1**
- Actually, all you really know are some buzz words. **-4**
- "Could you *paradigm-shift* the rolls over here?" **-22**
- "Wow! *Just-in-time* appetizers!" **-24**
- "Is anyone *claiming ownership* for this last breadstick?" **-34**
- You attempt a hostile takeover of the dessert tray. **-35**


- When you're picking up the tab for a client lunch, you always encourage your guest to order whatever she wants. **+3**
- You do the polite thing and make suggestions for her **+4**
- that way she can't order lobster. **-10**
- "Salads all around!" **-20**
- "Well, you said you wanted a 'lean and hungry' organization!" **-30**


- When you're the guest, you order a meal that's not too expensive. **+3**
- But then you figure, why not order something nice? **-5**

- When everyone else orders light pasta, you don't. **-21**
- The spotted owl could have used more coriander. **-121**


- During lunch, when important negotiations are taking place, you stick to one glass of wine and ice water. **+3**
- You decide maybe a couple of drinks would loosen you up **-4**
- and a little wine couldn't hurt. **-12**
- When the lunch is over, you can't remember what happened. **-45**
- You've got a room key in your pocket **-50**
- and a scar instead of a kidney. **-87**


- When you take a client out to lunch you realize you left your wallet back at the office. **-10**
- Your client offers to pay. **-2**
- You decline, and tell her you'll just go talk to the manager. **+1**
- You return to the table smiling, and say, "Well, at least that's settled!" **+3**
- "You wash, I dry!" **-45**


- When entertaining a client, you try to forge a bond of common interests. **+3**
- When a client says he's a big fan of the Audubon Society, you chime in with approval. **+3**
- You tell him you really love German cars, too. **-23**


- To ingratiate yourself with clients, you get involved in volunteer work and charity drives. **+4**
- You convince one client to donate hundreds of thousands of dollars to start up a bird sanctuary **+4**
- because you have a special concern for preserving wildlife **+5**
- and you've been aching to break out the twelve-gauge. **-33**

- At a posh event, you try to impress a client by discussing your ideas for the future growth of your company. **+4**
- You explain your brilliant concept for reconfiguring the five-year plan. **+4**
- He's extremely impressed. **+8**
- You realize you're sucking up to the wrong guy **-4**
- when he has to leave to refill the water glasses. **-33**

- You are invited to a corporate schmooze event by your boss **+3**
- and you come dressed in a nice dark suit and expensive tie. **+4**
- You come in a sport jacket, turtleneck, and your favorite well-worn khakis. **0**
- You come dressed in something you found on the bedroom floor. **-12**
- If anyone asks you tell them you really do play for Black Sabbath. **-30**

- At your boss's request, you take a client to a nightclub **+5**
- known for its "gentleman's entertainment." **-4**
- It's a topless club with women dancing on tables. **0**
- Your client is offended by the sexist environment. **-30**
- You try to make up for it by offering to perform a "Full Monty." **-98**
- You point out the fact that a place like this is good for women. **-33**
- You tell her there are no glass ceilings here **0**
- just glass tables. **0**
- "And, look! They're dancing on them!" **-45**

# 18 | DIRTY OFFICE TRICKS

In the workplace, there will always be employees far more competent than you. Therefore, it's up to you to level the playing field (without a backhoe, of course).

- When dealing with an angry client over the phone, you try to remain polite and accommodating, and respond quickly to his complaints. **+8**
- You put him on hold **-3**
- and hope he will hang up after ten minutes. **-6**
- You transfer the call to another coworker. **-8**
- You don't transfer the call to another coworker **-4**
- you just say *you're* another coworker **-10**
- one you really don't especially care for. **-10**
- "Yeah, this is BOB JONES, and maybe the reason you can't get your computer to recognize your printer is because you've got both of them plugged up your ass." **-28**
- You add, "Yes, I'll transfer you to my supervisor. Just tell her BOB JONES was happy to help." **-32**
- "And that BOB JONES offered you a free computer and free service for life!" **-54**

- When a serious problem arises at work, you issue a memo to your boss, claiming full responsibility. **+3**
- "I take full responsibility for that snafu in product fulfillment, and it will never happen again. Sincerely, Peter Moore." **+3**
- You issue a memo claiming to take responsibility—but not really. **-10**
- "I take full responsibility for that snafu in product fulfillment. I really should have been watching BOB JONES much more closely when he did the job." **-12**

- "Perhaps I wasn't clear in my instructions to BOB JONES. In the future, I will make it my responsibility to make sure BOB JONES never does this again. Sincerely, Peter Moore." **-45**
- "P.S. Is BOB JONES on or off the wagon these days?" **-65**

- When you're competing for a promotion with another equally qualified coworker, you concentrate on doing your best **+3**
- instead of undermining the other guy. **+5**
- When talking to the boss, you point out the positive attributes of the other coworker. **+9**
- You say he is a great guy and that you would do anything for him **+2**
- including cover for him **-5**
- when he has to leave early every day **-7**
- to see his court-ordered psychiatrist **-15**
- to deal with "those impulses." **-45**
- "He's been eating lightbulbs again." **-75**

- You're competing for a promotion with a coworker more qualified than you. **-6**
- You increase your chances by undermining his. **-7**
- You do this by taking credit for work he's done. **-10**
- When he comes up with a good idea, you claim he stole it from you. **-14**
- When he's on a sales call, you tell your boss you saw his car in the Hooters parking lot **-25**
- at 10 AM. **-40**
- You tell him the coworker meetings have been canceled when they haven't. **-12**
- When he goes to the bathroom, you turn off his office light and computer **-7**
- and tell everyone he went home early. **-19**

- "You know, he needs to get in those eighteen holes!" **-40**
- You make long-distance phone calls from his phone **-23**
- to cartels in Colombia **-56**
- you tip off the police **-55**
- then gladly volunteer to be a character witness at the hearing. **+5**

- You ingratiate yourself with your boss's spouse. **+2**
- If you win her over, you figure she'll say nice things to her husband **+4**
- which can only help your career. **+4**
- At social gatherings, you always chat her up. **+4**
- You and she become friends **+5**
- more than just friends. **-5**
- The boss doesn't suspect a thing **0**
- until you point out how lucky he is to be married to a natural blonde. **-354**

- You read up on the competition **+2**
- to help out your company **+9**
- to see if you can do better over there. **-6**
- You visit the competition. **-10**
- You promise that if they hire you, you'll feed them valuable secrets about your company. **-23**
- The special sauce: mayonnaise and ketchup! **-45**

- You volunteer for task forces and steering committees. **+2**
- It helps you get to know other people in the company **+3**
- which is clearly a boon to your Amway distributorship **-34**
- and your Mary Kay franchise. **-65**

- You often show up for work an hour or so late. **-8**
- But you make up for it by working late into the evening. **+3**
- You've found that's the best time to read everyone's mail **-11**
- and call your cousin in the Peace Corps **-20**

- in Sumatra **-34**
- and sit in the boss's chair **-34**
- and say, "Captain's Log, star date 2031. . . ." **-40**

# 19 | COVERING YOUR TRACKS

Everyone slacks off and makes horrible mistakes. But it takes a special kind of person to cover their tracks, and prevent the aftermath of suspensions, firings, lawsuits, and those bothersome parking lot switchblade fights.

- You're very late for a meeting. **-4**
- When you walk in, everybody scowls. **-6**
- You look at your watch, and say, "Oh! I must still be on London time!" **+2**
- You make a big show of resetting your watch **+3**
- and notice you're still wearing your golf glove. **-20**

- When your boss comes into your office and asks you where that big project is, you shrug and say, "Big project?" **-10**
- You say it's in the "Big Project Department." **-40**
- You ask, "You mean you didn't get my memo?" **-10**
- "I left it with your secretary." **-13**
- You add, "I think she may have a problem." **0**
- You make the guzzling-from-a-bottle motion. **-19**
- with the Scotch bottle from your desk. **-55**

- Your boss asks you for fresh, bold ideas for the upcoming advertising plan. **+2**
- You bring him a list of a dozen solid and impressive ideas. **+10**

- He realizes all the slogans sound familiar. -7
- "We try harder." -5
- "The quicker picker-upper." -6
- "Like a rock." -9
- You figure they fit perfectly for Viagra. -20

- It's a beautiful day, so you sneak out early from work. -4
- Your boss sees you in the parking lot and asks you where you're going. -15
- You tell her you're going to pick up your sick child. +5
- She knows you don't have children. -15
- You tell her it's a foster child +3
- and Sally Struthers demands that you fly to Bogota immediately. -32

- The boss walks into your office while you're at the *Penthouse* website. -3
- You click another window. 0
- It's another porno website. -5
- You tell him you're relieving stress -2
- and you can only do your best work when you're relaxed +1
- which explains why your pants are off. -40

- Your computer screen is filled with complex graphics. +2
- It's an outline for the big sales presentation. +4
- It's a downloaded picture of Jenny McCarthy -33
- naked -44
- actually, of Charlie McCarthy -87
- naked. -387

- You wander into work late. -4
- The boss catches you. -8
- She notices that you have neither showered nor shaved -11
- and that your clothes smell like booze -15

- and your eyes are bloodshot. **-19**
- She asks if you have a problem. **-20**
- You say, "Yes, the bars are closed." **-22**
- She asks you if you have a problem, and you blame it on the sales manager. **+4**
- You were out talking business with him last night **+3**
- and he likes to drink. **+2**
- Your boss points out that the sales manager is a recovering alcoholic. **-30**
- You reply, "Believe me, he has a long way to go!" **-50**

<br>

- You tell your boss that you'd like to enroll in continuing education courses **+1**
- to help improve your career skills **+3**
- which will make you a more valued employee **+2**
- so you can make a bigger contribution to the company. **+4**
- You just want to leave from work at 2:30 every Tuesday and Thursday **-6**
- just in time for *Jerry Springer*! **-23**
- When the boss asks you what courses you plan to take, you say those that directly benefit your job. **+2**
- You signed up for "Chinese Cooking for Beginners." **-4**
- You tell your boss there are great opportunities in Beijing. **-9**
- You sell paint. **-12**
- You never know when that Great Wall will need a new coat! **-40**

<br>

- The boss catches you walking out of the building with an armful of office supplies. **-20**
- You tell him you were planning on doing a lot of work over the weekend **+2**
- and this stuff will come in handy. **+3**
- You tell him you were taking these supplies back to Staples. **+3**
- You think the clerk made a mistake and overcharged the company. **+4**

- You say you smelled smoke, and thought it was important to save the fax machine. **-40**
- You tell him you're "walking the copier." **-50**

## HOW TO SPIN FOR SUCCESS

- You are summoned to make a presentation to the board of directors **+3**
- in which you're supposed to deliver bad news. **-4**
- But you put a positive spin on it. **+2**
- You say true, sales are down **-5**
- but at least that puts us in a lower tax bracket! **+1**
- You understand that everyone is alarmed over these losses **-5**
- but this is all part of your long-term strategy **+3**
- to lull the competition into a false sense of security! **-32**
- You admit there will have to be millions of dollars in product that will go unsold this year. **-4**
- But the company will save millions in taxes by donating much of this product to charity **+4**
- primarily, homeless shelters. **+5**
- You manufacture cellular phones. **-26**
- "Perfect for the person who has no home!" **-56**

- You decide to promote a new product with a celebrity endorser **+1**
- that regular people can identify with. **+3**
- You try to get someone highly esteemed and respectable. **+4**
- Like General Colin Powell or David Brinkley. **+5**
- They don't return your calls **-9**
- but Pauly Shore does. **-100**
- You insist he'll be a perfect match for your product **+2**
- which is disaster insurance **-34**
- after all, look at his career. **+12**

- When seeking out a celebrity endorser you decide to go hip. **+1**
- You want the whole campaign to be "edgy, extreme, and in-your-face." **-3**
- You sign up Yanni. **-34**
- You sign up the Red Hot Chili Peppers. **+10**
- Your client isn't excited. **-10**
- There just aren't a lot of Gen-Xers using Di-Gel. **-56**
- You tell them they will if they eat chili peppers! **-68**

- You work in public relations for a company with a lousy public persona **-5**
- the tobacco industry. **-10**
- You portray your company in a positive light **-5**
- by showing how smoking confers health benefits. **-13**
- "A pack a day deepens your voice." **-20**
- "Which is a tremendous benefit for sissy boys!" **-33**
- "Put a cigarette in your mouth, and your stuttering stops like that!" **-45**
- "Don't your lungs deserve that golden tan? We think so!" **-98**
- "Get your heart pumping without ever joining a gym!" **-75**
- "And remember, a hacking cough tightens your abs better than crunches!" **-85**

- You must face the media to discuss a serious problem that is clearly the fault of your company. **+1**
- You try to turn the error into something more positive. **+1**
- You admit that the chemical leaks have poisoned much of the water supply in the surrounding communities. **-45**
- You point out what a boon this will be to the funeral industry. **-98**
- You admit you're aware the beef your company sells may be contaminated by mad cow disease. **-20**
- But rather than recall any beef, you'd like you to focus on the positive **-3**

- and introduce the new corporate mascot. **-13**
- "Elsie, The Mad Cow!" **-145**
- "She's udderly infectious!" **-300**

# BUSINESS ABROAD

Here it pays to be on your toes. If you aren't, you'll be on your ass. And in one of those humid, mountaintop prisons made of bamboo (mmm . . . that doesn't sound half-bad . . . ).

- When eating at a formal dinner with foreign clients, you display your best manners. **+3**
- You compliment your hosts for an outstanding meal. **+7**
- You cough out the less than desirable elements into your cloth napkin. **-9**
- You skip the meal entirely. **-23**
- You brought your own **-30**
- from McDonald's. **-33**
- You say you gave up monkey brains for Lent. **-42**

- When greeting your hosts, you smile, bow, and thank them for their hospitality. **+3**
- You give them a firm handshake and pat them on the back. **-1**
- You give them a Dutch rub on the top of the head **-14**
- and call everyone Chief. **-35**
- You ask the German host where they kept Colonel Hogan. **-60**

- At the conclusion of difficult but highly successful negotiations, you emerge victorious. **+3**

- You humbly compliment your counterparts for their effective negotiating techniques. **+5**
- You jump up and down and chant "USA! USA!" **-20**

- To communicate with your hosts, you memorize key phrases in their language **+6**
- and learn the phonetic pronunciations of each of their names. **+10**
- You still say "I farted" instead of "I'm sorry." **-43**
- You admit that you don't know their language and rely solely on translators **-5**
- to help with greeting and pleasantries **+4**
- and tell the authorities you thought you were buying a real massage.

- During a meeting with your foreign counterparts, you listen intently, and speak only when you need to ask a question. **+10**
- You write secret messages in a notebook and pass occasional notes to your colleagues. **-6**
- "Check out Pol Pot over there at three o'clock." **-12**
- Instead of paying attention, you read the *USA Today International* sports page. **-40**
- You hum "America the Beautiful." **-30**
- When a conflict arises, you casually mention that the USA is the world's only remaining superpower. **-23**
- "And we can kick your third-world butt with a butter knife and a piece of string." **-33**
- You point out that they're damn lucky "we saved your ass in the war" **-34**
- to the Canadians **-121**
- who believe you. **+12**

- You enroll in a language class months ahead of time to prepare for your important trip to negotiate foreign rights in Japan. **+9**

- You buy cheap "Learn Japanese in Your Sleep" cassettes from an infomercial. **-12**
- You ask the Japanese dignitary about changes in trade barriers. **+3**
- But he hears, "Would you like a full body rub?" **-145**
- He does. **+10**
- You secure the biggest trade deal of the century. **+34**


- In your first meeting with Japanese businessmen, you extend your hand as a sign of greeting. **-8**
- He responds by bowing his head **0**
- which you shake vigorously. **-34**
- He kind of enjoys it. **+12**


- While traveling in foreign countries, you do your best to fit in **+2**
- and try not to act like "an ugly American." **+3**
- You greet your Russian hosts by calling them "comrades." **-13**
- You wear a Mao suit to Beijing. **-45**
- You ask the Saudis where they park the camels. **-55**
- You accuse your boss of stealing, just to see if they cut off his hands. **-65**
- They do. **-543**
- From now on you get to drive the rental. **+3**

# 21 | OFFICE TECHNOLOGY

Part of the fun of having a job is all the neat stuff you get to play with in the name of work. Whether it's a copier or a forklift, the possibilities for immense pleasure are endless, as well as the opportunities for trouble. After all, someone could lose an eye (or something far worse, if you get too close to the shredder).

## E-MAIL

- You like to end your sentence with cute little "emoticons" made from punctuation marks. **-3**
- You think this makes the office environment more friendly, and shows off your clever sense of humor. **-3**
  :) the happy face **-3**
  :( the sad face **-4**
  ;) the wink **-7**
  ;( the guy with pink eye **-9**
  .) the guy with one eye **-30**
  ) the smiling Stevie Wonder **-13**
  *:( the guy with the gaping head wound **-13**
  3> the hot receptionist on the twelfth floor **-14**
  :() Monica Lewinsky **-57**

- You refrain from abusing e-mail **+1**
- and only use it for business purposes. **+3**
- You use your e-mail to send out personal messages to friends at other companies. **-5**
- You send out dirty jokes **-10**
- and rumors about coworkers. **-20**
- You forward one to the wrong person **-22**
- your boss. **-33**
- Now he knows he should use a stronger deodorant **-98**
- and why his wife is always "working late." **-200**

## THE COPIER

The things you copy, and what they cost you:
- actual work documents **+3**
- your screenplay **-5**
- the invitations to your three-keg bash **-13**
- the chain letter you plan on sending throughout the company **-34**
- that really cute story from *Reader's Digest* **-54**
- your butt **-56**
- anything that requires fiddling with the magnifier, and making us wait **-12**
- the entry for the local poetry contest **-67**
- 300 copies of your resume **-100**
- and 300 copies of your cover letter **-100**
- which jams the copier **-125**
- which you had to bribe the copier repairman to fix. **-133**
- He won't take money **-19**
- but he will take a copy of your butt. **+12**

## YOUR PHONE AND VOICE MAIL

- You record a clear, succinct voice mail for your business phone. **+1**
- You record a voice mail that makes you sound very busy. **+1**
- "I'm not here right now, but I'll be checking my messages from the road" **+2**
- usually from a pay phone. **-4**
- You never know where the carnival will take you. **-57**

- To help out callers when you aren't at your phone, you leave a message to direct them to another live body. **+2**
- "If you need assistance, please call the receptionist." **+2**

- You are the receptionist. **-10**
- You disguise your voice **-12**
- as James Earl Jones **-33**
- as James Earl Ray. **-400**

- To give the impression that you're one busy fella, you often complain about the number of voice mails you get. **-2**
- "I've only been gone for a few hours, and I have eighteen voice mails!" **-3**
- You play them on the speakerphone. **-9**
- All of them are from your mom. **-33**
- You didn't make your bed again. **-45**

- You have a short, matter-of-fact voice mail greeting. **+1**
- You have a long and incredibly detailed greeting. **-2**
- You have created what you believe to be a humorous voice mail message. **-5**
- You pretend you are the President of the United States **-6**
- and you're just the Vice President. **-66**

- You answer your phone in a professional manner. **+4**
- You answer the phone in a lazy, couldn't-be-bothered voice. **-5**
- You pick up the phone only when you have nothing else to do. **-8**
- You put them on hold while you finish other business **-10**
- like that really challenging crossword puzzle **-17**
- or the first draft of your romance novel. **-50**
- You consider working for 911 just a temporary thing. **-130**

## YOUR COMPUTER EXPERTISE

- You like to call yourself a "webmaster." **-39**
- You walk around the office, talking in web-page lingo. **-55**
- "Dude, that's a stale or bale moment—nothing but fish food and dancing baloney." **-65**

- "Update your cobweb man, with that Kilroy you'll be 404 in no time." **-65**
- You don't actually own a computer **-100**
- but you still wear those carpal tunnel braces. **-150**

- You use computer jargon incessantly **-9**
- even when you aren't talking about computers. **-26**
- You talk about "interfacing" over espresso later **-27**
- and how much you'd like to check out a coworker's "mother-board." **-32**
- When you need to find the bathroom, it's to "download." **-76**
- "Boy, that took a lot of RAM." **-140**

## GADGETS

- You possess the latest in electronics and high tech office accessories. **-3**
- You like to show off the stuff to your coworkers. **-6**
- "This is my Datavac, which vacuums dust particles from my keyboard!" **-10**
- "It also makes a wonderful sex toy!" **-27**
- "This is my personal datapage organizer, which stores over 150,000 names of people, businesses, and government services in the surrounding 75 miles!" **-30**
- It's the local phone book. **-34**
- You show off your personal shredder, which allows you to destroy any high security document. **-40**
- It looks like a pair of scissors. **-50**
- You instruct people not to run while carrying them. **-55**

- You decide to purchase an expensive pen that also functions as a laser pointer. **-1**
- It projects a bright red dot **-2**
- that focuses on an object as much as fifty yards away. **-4**
- You rarely ever use the pointer in a work situation. **-4**

- Except when to aim it at a coworker's forehead **-9**
- and say, "Look, Thompson's from Pakistan!" **-54**

 # HOW DO YOU LOOK?

Not good, if you're reading this book.

## CORPORATE ATTIRE

- You dress exceptionally well at work. **+3**
- You wear crisp white shirts, expensive ties, and shined shoes. **+4**
- You dress better than all of your coworkers. **+1**
- You dress better than your boss **-6**
- who knows it **-8**
- because everybody points it out to him **-10**
- including you **-12**
- when you offer to take him shopping **-32**
- at Wal-Mart. **-50**

- You come to work dressed in a tasteful suit and tie. **+4**
- By 9:30 AM the jacket is already off. **-2**
- By 9:45 the tie has been loosened. **-4**
- By 11:30 you've rolled up your sleeves **-6**
- and unbuttoned the top few buttons of your shirt. **-8**
- And you haven't even finished with the sports page. **-12**
- By then you're in only your boxers **-43**
- the ones with "ventilation." **-98**

- You wear ties that are rather conservative, nothing too out-landish. **+2**
- You like to wear ties that are extremely colorful, even wild. **-4**

- You wear ties that have more personality than you do -8
- which is easy to do. -10
- You think your Jerry Garcia ties are especially "edgy" -13
- and you've always loved his ice cream. -34

- You wear tweed. -4
- You wear tweed and you're not a professor. -5
- You wear a bow tie -4
- and you're not George Will. -8
- Okay, you are George Will. -23
- You wear short-sleeved dress shirts with a tie -13
- and you've got really hairy forearms -34
- and don't repair copiers. -45
- You wear slacks with dress shoes +3
- athletic shoes -9
- horseshoes -90
- clown shoes. -198
- You wear running shoes because you jog at lunch. 0
- No, because they're the only pair of shoes you own -28
- which, judging by the flies in your office, is obvious. -56

## YOUR BRIEFCASE

- You carry a new leather briefcase that exudes smooth professionalism. +3
- You carry a scuffed leather case that suggests a home-grown sensibility. +3
- You think your briefcase tells everyone that you're really dedicated +4
- or you wouldn't feel the need to carry around your work. 0
- If work is what you have in there -4

- besides your gym clothes **-5**
- the Nintendo **-7**
- the miniature television. **-30**
- You never know when there'll be a special episode of *Touched by an Angel*. **-35**

## CASUAL FRIDAY

- When your company institutes Casual Fridays, you don't pay much attention. **+2**
- You think it's a great idea **-2**
- because now you get to show everyone "the real you." **-5**
- Break out the puka shells! **-34**
- You wear camouflage **-13**
- with your "David Koresh Was Right" T-shirt. **-20**

- You wear clothing that reflects your heritage. **-3**
- You wear the headdress. **-23**
- You slap on your chain mail. **-98**
- You've got the leather dog collar on **-134**
- it matches your bullwhip **-300**
- and people still don't notice you. **-231**
- Maybe you should get out of San Francisco. **0**

- You go out and get a special wardrobe just for Casual Fridays. **-5**
- You lay out your clothes the night before. **-9**
- You actually have an "outfit." **-44**
- It took forever to find a crop top that matches the hot pants **-98**
- and still shows off your tattoo of Menudo. **-121**

# 23 | THE PROCRASTINATION PRIMER

Why do we put off doing stuff? Good question. For the most part, it boils down to one central theme . . . Hey, isn't *Ricki Lake* on now?

# 24 | THE PROCRASTINATION PRIMER (AGAIN)

Why do we put off doing stuff? Good question. For the most part, it boils down to one central theme: maybe the assignment just isn't worth doing in the first place.

- You're overwhelmed by the immensity of an assignment. **-2**
- You divide the task into small parts and work on it incrementally. **+5**
- You wait until the day before it's due to get started **-20**
- then fake an aneurism. **-45**
- By now the paramedics know your deadlines better than you do. **-98**

- The assignment has no prospect of immediate benefits. **0**
- You build in your own motivation. **+8**
- You wait until keeping your job becomes your motivation **-30**
- then you blame everything on El Niño. **-45**

- When faced with a new assignment, you just don't know where to start. **-2**

- So you break down the task into incremental steps **+4**
- and step one is: Have a donut **-14**
- step two is: Have another donut **-15**
- and a glass of milk. **-17**
- Step three: repeat previous steps until covered in your own sick. **-50**

- You have a great lack of enthusiasm for the project. **-5**
- You create a work-friendly environment. **+5**
- But you do nothing until the boss asks for a progress report. **-9**
- Then you say you hit your head **-13**
- on your new ergonomic light fixture. **-34**
- You say you feel dizzy. **-40**
- Then you ask him for a piggyback ride. **-75**
- He gives you one. **+3**

- When faced with a large project, you refrain from engaging in busy work. **+3**
- Actually, you find new things to clean in your office **-9**
- and in coworkers' offices, too. **-24**
- You adjust the color of your computer desktop **-13**
- and try out a succession of screen savers. **-15**
- You start fixing things that really don't need fixing. **-10**
- It takes you three hours to untangle the phone cord **-10**
- and another two hours to shape it into a turban. **-32**

- You begin a task the very moment it is assigned. **+3**
- You let the idea "gestate" until you feel ready to proceed. **0**
- You decide to do a little "preliminary research" before you get under way. **-10**
- You think it might be wise to "sleep on it" before you make any rash commitments. **-15**
- Then you're ready. **+1**
- "Okay, you want extra foam on that latte?" **-42**
- Not bad for an MBA. **-45**

# 25 | HOW ANNOYING ARE YOU?

The points you earn or lose often have nothing to do with your productivity or talent. In fact, one might say the majority of all scoring opportunities come in the daily activities that occur outside actual work. Which, you know, comprises about 97 percent of the work day—give or take a nap.

- You rarely engage in playful roughhousing in the hallways. **+3**
- Once in a while you punch someone in the shoulder as they walk by **-1**
- and say, "Dude, what's up?" **-3**
- You high five others during meetings **-3**
- and say, "Dude, don't leave me hanging!" **-10**
- You often put fellow employees in playful headlocks **-7**
- and give him "noogies" **-8**
- or give *her* "noogies" **-19**
- or wedgies. **-45**
- You think this horseplay lightens an employee's mood. **-14**
- Tell that to the guy on the ventilator. **-65**

- You use phrases at work like:
- "Don't even go there." **-4**
- "Been there, done that." **-9**
- "You go girl." **-13**
- You snap your fingers and wave your hand when you do that **-15**
- and you're a middle-aged white guy **-23**
- but you're really into Puff Daddy **-33**
- which explains the Glock 9-millimeter. **-143**

- You're the king of arcane facts. **-12**
- You bore everyone with the fluctuation of Mike Schmidt's batting average from 1973 to 1979 **-30**
- followed by the migration patterns of Siberian snow geese. **-34**
- But when the boss asks you about some simple budget numbers, you fall silent. **-44**
- You tell him you'll get back to him. **-9**
- You're too busy alphabetizing your favorite quotes from Captain Picard. **-98**

- You often call a younger employee "college boy" **-8**
- because he went to some Ivy League school **-12**
- and has "one of them fancy diplomas" on the wall. **-14**
- You call him "junior" because he's much younger than you. **-10**
- You call him "son" because he's a lot younger than you. **-13**
- You have to call him "boss" because you should have gone to college. **-30**

- You like to show your coworkers pictures once you get them developed **-3**
- pictures of some wedding you went to **-4**
- or your child's birthday **-4**
- with kids smearing cake on their faces **-6**
- or some vacation at Club Med **-12**
- where your thong turned your ass into two uncooked hams **-20**
- or the pictures of your cat hanging playfully from the drapes. **-32**
- In fact, you show many pictures of your cats **-43**
- but none of your children **-56**
- you call your cats "your children" **-98**
- which explains their diapers. **-165**

- You go for that graduate degree to help improve your career opportunities. **+3**

- You choose an area of study that will make you more valuable as an employee. **+3**
- You get a Ph.D. in something useful, like electrical engineering or economics. **+5**
- You get a Ph.D. in "Human Change" **-19**
- from the "Healing Institute of Modern Empowerment" **-45**
- in Grenada. **-55**
- Yet you insist everyone call you "doctor" **-10**
- even when we ask you for more cracked pepper on our salads. **-45**

- You assert your individuality in the workplace. **+1**
- You like to think of yourself as an "independent thinker" **-3**
- or better, a "rebel." **-8**
- You tell everyone how you're not just a corporate guy. **-2**
- You refer to employees above you as "the suits." **-2**
- You really hate those lifeguards. **-34**

- You often say to people, "Hey, I'm not just a bean counter." **-3**
- You work for Arthur Andersen. **-5**
- You work for Van Camp's **-13**
- counting beans. **-43**

- At work, you decide to differentiate yourself from the crowd **+2**
- through your appearance. **-2**
- You get an earring, because you think it makes you look dangerous **-4**
- as you drive to work in your Dodge Caravan **-10**
- with the "Honor Student Aboard" bumper sticker. **-12**
- You decide to get a tattoo **-12**
- on your bicep. **-13**
- It's a skull. **-14**
- You think it intimidates people **-15**
- which could explain why your tip jar is empty. **-43**

- When you're out with friends, you often complain about your job. **-4**
- You whine incessantly about the hours, the lack of pay, the crummy conditions. **-9**
- You're chief taster for Häagen Dazs. **-14**
- You're the airbrush guy at *Penthouse*. **-32**
- You're a sand remover for the *Sports Illustrated* Swimsuit Issue. **-34**
- "It's a pain using my tongue to get in the hard-to-reach places." **-40**

- You're always cordial to new employees. **+2**
- You're a new employee's best pal **-5**
- because you're just a friendly person. **+3**
- because the rest of the staff can't stand you **-19**
- and the only way to make friends is to glom onto new employees **-20**
- who don't know much about you **-4**
- until they see the bootlegged "break room" video. **-198**

- You often borrow a coworker's car **-5**
- because yours is always "in the shop." **-15**
- You take the car on many odd errands. **-8**
- You return the car in the same condition as when you borrowed it. **0**
- You always leave something behind **-9**
- a coffee stain in the front seat **-11**
- a cigarette burn in the upholstery **-13**
- a large dent in the driver-side door **-19**
- an article of dirty clothing **-20**
- the floor plan to a bank and a couple of ski masks **-165**
- an odd, lingering smell emanating from the trunk **-222**
- you had to put that damn guard somewhere. **-234**

- You try not to bother fellow employees while they work. **+2**
- You often enter their offices unannounced **-5**
- to recount the movie you rented last night. **-5**
- The movie stars Billy Crystal **-12**
- actually, it's a foreign film **-14**
- it's a coming-of-age film **-20**
- it's three hours long **-25**
- or at least it takes you that long to tell us about it. **-34**
- When you're done, you say, "Enough chatting. Get back to work." **-35**
- You stop at another cubicle and start all over again. **-40**
- This time the movie stars James Spader. **-335**

- When you jam the copier, you do your best to fix it. **+3**
- When you break the copier, you notify the service department promptly. **+4**
- When you jam the copier, you slink away and let someone else deal with it. **-5**
- You walk away, but not before putting a sign on the copier, telling everyone it's broken **0**
- "Please don't use me. I'm not working!" **-12**
- Your boss hangs the same sign on you. **-30**

- You don't spend your time in the office annoying employees **+3**
- or walking around **+4**
- or getting coffee refills **+3**
- or using the bathroom. **-20**
- After all, that's what your "Employee of the Month" trophy is for. **-156**

- When you've got the sniffles, you don't make a big deal out of it. **0**
- When you've got the sniffles, you spend the entire day complaining about how sick you feel **-5**

- but you won't go home **-8**
- you'd rather impress the boss by "sticking it out" **-12**
- and giving everyone else what you have. **-14**
- Who knew TB could spread so quickly! **-200**

- You run a side business out of your office. **-33**
- It's Mary Kay. **-9**
- You're running a booming business **0**
- as your productivity sucks. **-34**
- You can't understand why your coworkers are upset **-35**
- as you try to spritz them with fragrance samples when they come in the front door. **-54**

- You strike up a conversation with your boss in the gym locker room. **+2**
- You attempt informal, guy-type banter. **-4**
- "Hey, you've got some great quads!" **-10**
- "Check out those awesome hamstrings!" **-15**
- "Mind if I use your roll-on?" **-13**
- "Towel fight!" **-20**
- "You know, surgery can straighten that." **-45**

# 26 | THE PECULIARITIES OF OFFICE LIFE

Here's a whole bunch of stuff that happens at work, but nothing that really deserves an individual chapter. So we threw 'em all together right here, under the heading "The Peculiarities of Office Life." Isn't that clever? Haven't you done that before?

## YOUR WORKLIFE FANTASIES

- You daydream at your desk when work is slow. **-3**
- You daydream when a coworker is discussing her "personal problem" with you. **-5**
- You daydream during long meetings. **-6**
- You daydream even in the midst of doing serious work **-10**
- which could explain all the sponges left in your patients. **-455**

- You daydream that you have secret, superhuman powers. **-3**
- One of them involves lightning-speed collating. **-45**
- You daydream about heroically saving your boss's life in a fire **-3**
- as you let your coworkers perish. **-24**
- Serves them right for making fun of your haircut. **-50**

- You daydream about having a clever answer for everything **-15**
- and impressing everyone with your quick wit. **-15**
- When someone really asks you a question, you stammer and sputter **-30**
- because you are too busy daydreaming **-35**
- about having a clever answer for everything. **-45**

- You daydream about asking for a raise **+1**
- and telling off your boss when he rejects your plea. **-3**
- "You can take this job and . . . oh, never mind." **-12**
- You daydream about giving the janitor a piece of your mind **-9**
- then making up with the janitor **-14**
- and becoming great pals. **-30**
- He lets you try on his tool belt! **-43**
- You daydream about sleeping with the intern. **-3**
- But then again, so does everyone else **+3**
- except she's *not* their cousin. **-34**

## HANDLING CUSTOMER COMPLAINTS

- When documenting a complaint, you have the person describe the exact problem. **+3**
- You listen quietly and express empathy when appropriate. **+1**
- You forget to pick the phone back up when she's through. **-9**
- You react positively and try not to be defensive. **+2**
- You tell them to call a therapist. **-8**
- You restate all the specific facts as you understand them **+2**
- and summarize the problem for them. **+3**
- "So basically you're a nitwit." **-9**
- You ask the customer exactly what is needed to correct the situation. **+1**
- You respond, "I'll take care of it." **+3**
- "When I'm good and ready." **-8**
- You tell the customer exactly what action you're going to take after you get off the phone. **+3**
- "I'm going to make fun of you with my coworkers." **-15**
- "Then have another donut." **-19**
- You thank the customer for taking the time to express his concerns **+3**
- then offer him solace **+4**
- and add that you really don't work here. **-12**

### THE USES AND ABUSES OF INTERNS

So here's how you score when you have your intern:
- look for something you lost **-4**
- in your trash can **-5**
- in the Dumpster **-22**
- in a seedy bar across town **-34**
- in your pants **-432**

- act as your personal errand boy **-34**
- act as a dummy for your own personal CPR class **-44**
- dress up as your ex-girlfriend **-49**

- label your files **-2**
- label your office furniture **-5**
- label your body parts **-40**
- label your underwear **-132**

- research the names of your client's family members **-3**
- research your family tree **-43**
- prune your family's tree **-54**
- alphabetize the CD collection on your bookshelf **-3**
- alphabetize your clippings of Siegfried and Roy articles **-40**

- photocopy the phone book because there's only one in the office **-9**
- and it's too far away from your desk **-27**
- track down the cheapest place in town to get your car washed **-10**
- make him wash the car anyway **-32**

- remove the pickles from your tuna fish sandwich (after all, you said *no* pickles) **-12**
- remove the poppy seeds from your bagel **-211**
- and then count them up to keep her busy **-321**

- return videos to Blockbuster so you don't have to pay a late fee **-12**
- have her pick up another selection while she's there **-13**
- it's something so embarrassing you can't get it yourself **-17**
- meaning, it stars Barbra Streisand **-43**

- put together your new multifunctional desk **-14**
- carry it up to your seventeenth-floor office **-50**
- pick up your dry-cleaning **-16**
- pick up your sister from band practice **-33**
- in Canton, Ohio **-500**

- have her pick up a package **-4**
- on the corner of 43rd and 8th **-54**
- have her drop off an envelope at the same place **-98**
- tell her to check for cops **-123**
- tell her to lie to the cops **-403**
- tell her to aim low when firing **-799**

- pick up stuff at the drugstore **-13**
- pick up embarrassing stuff at the drugstore **-21**
- make her return the embarrassing stuff **-32**
- because you specifically said "lubricated" **-43**

## TAKE YOUR DAUGHTERS TO WORK DAY

- Tomorrow is "Take Your Daughter to Work Day," and you decide to help prepare in case any of the employees' daughters are brought around. **+4**
- You clean up your office. **+1**
- You put away the blow-up doll. **+3**
- You forget to take down the calendar. **-34**
- You explain that "stacked and packed" is a term to describe an efficient filing system. **-33**
- You write up a little presentation **+2**
- to explain to the children exactly what you do. **+3**
- Which is, "sit around and look busy." **-45**

- "And yell at your mother for being late." **-54**
- You have candy at your desk for the kids when they stop by. **+2**
- And a bottle of Scotch for yourself when they leave. **-76**

## LUNCH AT THE OFFICE

- You keep your lunch in the office refrigerator. **0**
- You actually put your name on the container **-3**
- as if you think someone might actually steal it **-11**
- but not everyone feels as strongly about Spaghettios as you do. **-17**
- When you eat at your desk, you always make sure to toss the leftovers immediately **+4**
- which is why you lobbied so hard for a window office. **-19**
- The pizza you order always comes with a number of greasy toppings **-4**
- afterward, so do your memos. **-14**
- You leave wrappers, empty cans, and dirty napkins around your office. **-3**
- You sometimes leave a half-eaten sandwich in a drawer in case you get hungry later. **-8**
- You then forget about it for months. **-28**
- But even then, it still tastes pretty good. **-134**

## YOUR PERSONAL ERRAND SCORECARD

Here's how you score when you use work time for:
- hitting the drugstore **-2**
- knocking off the drugstore **-321**
- getting an oil change **-4**
- getting a sex change **-543**
- picking up groceries **-3**

- picking up a runaway **-43**
- leaving her in the trunk while you work **-400**
- dropping off your dry-cleaning **-3**
- picking up your dry-cleaning **-4**
- picking up the dry-cleaner **-43**
- heading to the gym to work out **-5**
- heading to the parking lot to make out **-43**
- meeting with your therapist **-3**
- meeting with your bartender **-43**
- returning a movie **-1**
- renting a movie **-2**
- making a movie **-34**
- in a local motel **-76**
- the runaway has a featured role **+10**

## EXCUSES, EXCUSES

You need to leave work early because of:
- serious back pain **+1**
- serious back spasms **+2**
- a serious backgammon tournament on ESPN 2 **-35**

- you've got painful headaches **+3**
- you're experiencing severe migraines **+6**
- you're suffering severely hurt feelings **-45**
- you're still upset over the death of Princess Diana **-55**

- sniffles **-4**
- bad cough **+1**
- a really bad cough **+2**
- a really bad acid flashback **-13**
- and you have to land the plane **-632**

- your astigmatism is acting up **+3**
- no, make that your stigmata **-122**
- those red Magic Markers really come in handy **-187**

- illness in the family **+4**
- death in the family **+9**
- multiple deaths in the family **+13**
- and you need a little time to get your passport in order **-593**

- car trouble **-2**
- a minor car accident **+7**
- a major car accident **+12**
- you were severely injured **+23**
- but you'll be back at work in the morning, pronto **-33**
- if anyone asks, you got that golden tan waiting for the paramedics **-140**

# 27 | YOUR WORKPLACE ATTITUDE

A good attitude is more than just wearing a smile and donning fresh, clean underwear. It's a reflection on your willingness to work hard, take risks, and accept new challenges. It's also a handy thing to harp on when you can't give out raises ("Your work has been fine, Johnson, but what bothers us is your attitude").

- You always do your best work, whether the boss is in the office or out of town. **+2**
- You only do real work when you know the boss is lurking about. **-20**

- Then you make a lot of productive noise. -23
- You shout, "I've got a buyer on line eight!" -6
- Your phone only has one line. -35

- You listen to the Tony Robbins tapes your boss gave you. +3
- You start to think Tony might have some useful things to say. -15
- Now you actually quote him at work -45
- while pumping your fists in the air. -89
- Your passenger decides to get into another cab. -121

- You like to exercise with your coworkers. +2
- It builds a sense of camaraderie. +2
- You organize post-work volleyball games +1
- and weekend "fun runs." +3
- You lead your coworkers in a stress-reducing regimen of yoga and tantric breathing exercises +3
- as well as Transcendental Meditation -3
- during the strategic planning meeting. -45
- You levitate to get a better view of the pie charts. -55

- To upgrade your image, you volunteer for the company's charity program. +1
- You organize the clothing drive for the homeless. +6
- You walk around telling everyone about it. -9
- You didn't have to +1
- because everyone recognized the boss's old sportcoat. -34

- In order to improve your efficiency at work, you take some continuing education courses. +5
- You take a two-week time management course +7
- which makes you miss a critical deadline -15
- by two weeks. -50

- When you get angry, you learn to communicate your disapproval appropriately. +2

- You've even enrolled in an anger management course **+2**
- to help you channel your emotions more effectively. **+5**
- You have learned a great deal from that course. **+8**
- So much so, you've held onto the three-ring orientation binder. **+4**
- It scares the hell out of everyone when you hurl it across the hall. **-30**

- You never call in sick unless you absolutely have to. **+4**
- When you call in sick, mysteriously it's always on a Friday or a Monday. **-8**
- You put on a well-honed "sick" voice **-10**
- and your special "cough." **-12**
- The boss can still hear the announcer in the background yell, "They're off!" **-44**

- You help bolster the reputation and image of your company in the community **+5**
- through well-publicized charity work **+12**
- and frequent appearances on local television **+13**
- with local law enforcement **+4**
- with your jacket pulled over your head. **-75**

## YOUR OFFICE TALENTS

- You are the designated pro at repairing office equipment. **+4**
- When the copier is jammed you know where to check **+3**
- or at least, where to kick. **-3**
- When the fax ink runs dry, you know exactly how to refill it. **+3**
- You ask one of your overworked secretaries to do it. **-3**
- When the office printer jams, you figure out the problem on your own. **+4**
- Next time, don't put centerfolds into the automatic feeder. **-23**

- You pride yourself on instituting change within the company. **+4**
- Others call it bankruptcy, you call it change. **-43**
- You can point to many projects your company started because of you **+9**
- like the new recycling plan **+3**
- like the special "quit smoking" and "lose weight" programs **+4**
- because you're the only fat smoker in the company. **-34**
- You're also responsible for the recent installation of security cameras in the cafeteria. **-10**
- Now you're going to have to go out and buy your own silverware. **-40**


- You volunteer to take charge of various extracurricular activities **+3**
- like coordinating the softball team, the office picnic, and chartered trips to museums. **-3**
- You consider yourself the company "funmeister" **-15**
- because you take special pride in bringing fun to the workplace **-4**
- because you find these duties far easier than actually doing your real job. **-23**
- But no one really knows what that is anyway **-43**
- which is good, since you're in charge of downsizing. **-123**


- To protect yourself against being fired, you take on unique responsibilities to create a special niche for yourself. **+4**
- You're the designated fire marshal. **-30**
- Nice orange vest! **-34**
- You become privy to knowledge that makes you indispensable to the company. **+3**
- You're the only employee who knows the four-digit code to the alarm system **-30**

- which helps when you need new furniture for your apartment. **-98**

- You enroll in self-improvement courses at work **+3**
- including the company CPR class. **+1**
- But you give up because you don't like the practice dummies. **-3**
- You're thrown out because you liked one of them too much. **-34**
- As the framed picture on your desk can attest. **-444**

---

### THE ALL-TIME POINT LOSER AT WORK

- being the only guy in the office invited to a baby shower **-3789**

# CONCLUSION: YOUR SCORECARD TOTALS

Put down your pencils (or pens, depending on what you stole from the supply closet). It is that special time when we must tally up your score. Remember to tabulate your numbers honestly. You're only fooling yourself if you exaggerate your score, and you'll further delude yourself into thinking you really deserve a corner office (or, at least another donut). Sit down, crack open a beer, and put up your feet (oh, and close your office door, if you have one).

**500 points or more:** Well done. We see a smooth road ahead, filled with raises, promotions, and illicit affairs with bright-eyed interns. Of course, with such a high point total, you're in danger of alienating all of your coworkers, who by now, probably hate you enough as it is (note: if you've already won "Employee of the Year," you might want to check your brake cables). To ease the minds of fellow employees, pull a diversionary tactic: come to work with a mohawk and a ferret. That'll knock you down a rung.

**250 to 500 points:** Good work. You've got enough points to keep you moving up the ladder, and not quite enough to incite thoughts of revenge among your coworkers. Meaning, they won't urinate in your coffee. Keep this hearty bank account up, and you should be afforded more than enough leeway to take afternoons off to play golf, go skiing, or just sit quietly in your small apartment scratching yourself (tell me about it).

**0 points:** It sounds bad, but hey, join the club. This is where most of us are in cubicle land—with our heads a little above water and our bosses breathing down our necks. You can obviously do much better, however. Why not start by getting rid of those empty minibar bottles in your desk drawer?

**-250 points:** Deep doo-doo. You might consider dusting off your resume, or perhaps your passport. Keep up this sorry display, and soon you'll be demoted to some menial detail, probably involving the use of disinfectants and rubber gloves. But maybe you're into that sort of thing (not that we aren't!).

**-500 points:** Quit your job immediately. Apparently the working life is not suitable for you. Find another way to while away the hours instead. We suggest something that is taxing to neither the brain nor the body. Have you ever considered becoming a management consultant?